THE
LA FENICE
COOKBOOK

LUIGI'S PASSION

Luigi Orgera and *Sally Doulis*

with Colleen Mathieu

McArthur & Company

Toronto

First published in Canada in 2001 by
McArthur & Company
322 King Street West, Suite # 402
Toronto, Ontario, Canada, M5V 1J2

National Library of Canada Cataloguing in Publication Data

Orgera, Luigi

The La Fenice cookbook : Luigi's passion

ISBN 1-55278-197-6

1. Cookery, Italian. I. Doulis, Sally. II. Mathieu,
Colleen, 1942- . III. Title.

TX723.O73 2001   641.5945   C2001-930226-6

Recipes and original paintings by: Luigi Orgera
Dessert recipes by: Alessandra Orgera
Recipes compiled by: Sally Doulis
Wine consultant: Adriano Vicentini
Recipes tested by: Colleen Mathieu

Cover and interior design and typesetting:
    Counterpunch / Peter Ross
Index: Barbara Schon
Printed and bound in Canada by Transcontinental Printing Inc.

The publisher would like to acknowledge the financial support
of the Government of Canada through the Book Publishing
Industry Development Program (BPIDP) for our publishing
activities. The publisher further wishes to acknowledge the
financial support of the Ontario Arts Council for our publishing program.

10 9 8 7 6 5 4 3 2 1

This book is published in memory of Luigi Orgera, his life and his food.

CONTENTS

PREFACE

These are the recipes of a professional chef known by Torontonian gourmands and others for his outstanding Italian cuisine – Luigi Orgera, executive chef/owner, of La Fenice Ristorante. In April 2000, just as this book was nearing completion, Luigi was diagnosed with leukemia. On September 20, 2000, Luigi died, just four days before his 67th birthday. This book is a tribute to his spirit and we hope that it will help to keep his memory alive.

Luigi's spirit and contribution to food culture were previously recognized in June, 1997, at the Quirinale (the President's Palace) in Rome, when the President of the Republic of Italy presented to Luigi a bronze plaque and a "Pergamena" honoring La Fenice Ristorante as an Ambassador of Culture for its authenticity of Italian cuisine outside Italy. Then, in September, 1997, La Fenice was the recipient of the prestigious DiRoNA Award, and is now listed in "The Guide to Distinguished Restaurants of North America". Distinguished Restaurants of North America is a non-profit organization sponsored by companies interested in culinary and hospitality excellence. It promotes quality of food and presentation. La Fenice is a warranted recipient.

Over the twenty-odd years that I have observed Luigi's restaurant, it has flourished in good times and bad. While stars of the culinary trade have risen and fallen, bringing impecunious times to their backers, La Fenice has persevered.

When I first met my husband, Alex, he had a peculiar rigidity about experimenting with restaurants; he would not venture to those unfamiliar. His thesis was that having once discovered a suitable hospice for his palate, it was dangerous and possibly unfaithful to consider other sources of satisfaction. (Fortunately this thesis also applied to his marriage!) Then, one night, a friend insisted that we try La Fenice. My dear husband was faced with the conflict to either remain steadfast in his beliefs or venture his palate and appease a friend. Fortunately, he agreed to experiment and to his astonishment and disbelief he enjoyed an extraordinary meal. After careful consideration he asked to speak to the chef. When he met Luigi, he inquired whether there was a second mortgage on the restaurant. When it was admitted that in fact there was, Alex informed Luigi that he would endeavor to eat his way through that indebtedness. Thus, Alex's rigidity prevailed, but then La Fenice became his favorite restaurant.

For the next several years, Alex, who was in the investment business, took his clients and colleagues to lunch almost daily to La Fenice and when we married, Luigi opened up his restaurant on a Sunday afternoon so that we could celebrate with our friends in proper gastronomic fashion.

Luigi Orgera was born in 1933 in a small town, Spigno Saturnia, Latina, Italy (seventy miles south of Rome on the west coast of Italy, the district known as Lazio). Luigi was the sixth child in a family of eight. His family was in the restaurant and hotel business and as a young boy he learned the trade. His cooking talents were inspired by his mother's superior skills and the professional chefs employed by the family. To say the family fell on hard times during World War II is an understatement. The entire village was bombed and they lost their homes and businesses. They literally ran for their lives. The family escaped from the dangers of war by fleeing to the hills and there they stayed for two years, 1943 and 1944, until the war was over. After the war, with the help of the Italian government and the USA Marshall Plan, the family rebuilt their business and "rose from the ashes." (The name of the restaurant, La Fenice, means "The Phoenix", i.e., the bird that rises from its own ashes.) Luigi was ten to twelve years old during those devastating times. He went on to complete high school and afterwards he enrolled in a fashion design course in Prato, Italy. He had always had a passion for the arts and he hoped to become a professional

*Oil painting of Luigi's
village, right.
Abstract water colour
painting, below.*

designer. As a child he loved drawing and music. He played the organ, piano and mandolin. Of course, the churches in Italy are well known for their art treasures and involvement with music over the centuries. Luigi played the organ at the local church and was known as a director of plays put on through the church social group.

Luigi's first dream, that of being a professional designer, was substituted for another, more immediate love, his childhood sweetheart, the lovely Alessandra (Sandra). He met Alessandra not in high school, but in kindergarten! Thus, they had been through many emotional experiences together. Alessandra's family was also a victim of the war years. Her family, too, fled to the mountains and lived there for two years. Her father was a skilled cabinet-maker and out of dire necessity he designed and built a portable stone mill in which to grind wheat for the entire community and feed his family of seven. The mill itself was such a specialized piece of equipment, there was even a mechanism to regulate the thickness of the wheat. Today, the mill is in Luigi and Alessandra's home in Toronto. When Alessandra was a teenager, her parents decided to leave Italy and emigrate to Canada. So what was the romantic eighteen-year-old, Luigi, to do? He followed his heart. Alessandra's love came through and she sponsored her fiancé to emigrate to Canada (an immigration requirement back in 1953). Luigi prepared himself for emigration by studying English, and after two years he was welcomed into Canada.

Luigi did not cook immediately, however. With an entrepreneurial spirit, he got a real estate license, opened up a few barbershops, and went to work for Seagrams as a wine representative (thus, Luigi's superior knowledge of wine). Just eight years later, in 1961, inspired by the lack of authentic Italian cuisine in Toronto, Luigi opened his first restaurant on the Queensway. It was called

Milano, 1975 (left).
Just married January,
1954 (below).

Latina, named after his Italian province. In 1967, Luigi took in a partner and they ran the restaurant until 1983. In 1973, Luigi, his partner and other investors opened La Cantinetta, a 300 seat restaurant on the north side of King Street at John. La Cantinetta was designed by Barton Myers and Jack Diamond, leading architects in Toronto at the time. Perhaps the vision was to provide a large restaurant, like so many in Italy, where entire families and friends could meet and experience the wonderful food of the Italian homeland. La Cantinetta was sold in 1981.

Luigi had other plans. He opened La Fenice Ristorante in 1984, under his sole proprietorship.

La Fenice was inspired by the continuing unavailability of quality Italian food in Toronto. Most people still came to Italian restaurants to eat spaghetti and meatballs and pizza. Luigi wanted to introduce the populace to grilled fish and seafood, the fare of the coastal cities of Italy. Luigi was a busy restauranteur and an accomplished artist. When you visit his simple, yet elegant, restaurant, you will see his substantial, colorful paintings decorating the walls. Luigi depended on his longtime, loyal staff and his wife, Alessandra, creator of the excellent desserts for the restaurant.

Luigi and Alessandra have two children, a son and a daughter, and three grandchildren who retain extended family ties. In true Mediterranean style, Luigi made sure he kept family relationships alive: his whole family came to North America except one sister, who remained in Italy on the family property to grow, harvest, and produce some of the best olive oil in the world. Where do you think Luigi's special olive oil comes from? Lazio, of course.

A NOTE ON INGREDIENTS

Luigi Orgera believed that the finest, freshest ingredients make for the most delicious results. La Fenice is justifiably famous for the special extra virgin olive oil that Luigi imported from his hometown, Spigno Saturnia. Although Luigi insisted on extra virgin olive oil for all of the cooking at his restaurant, the "special" oil is used where it can be best appreciated – on fresh tomatoes, carpaccio, mozzarella and even on bread. In fact, the oil is so superb that people have been known to eat it by the spoonful.

Not only did Luigi import the oil, he helped to make it. Every other year, the Gaeta olives are harvested in January. When the biannual crop was ready, Luigi went to Italy. The olives he used are grown without pesticides, picked by hand, milled on stone, cold-pressed and filtered by hand – the way fine olive oil has been made for centuries. This is not simply because Luigi and his family were preserving tradition; olive oil is very sensitive to heat and the olives are easily bruised. Careful handling ensures that the oil is top-quality.

Once the oil is filtered, it is stored in Luigi's sister's wine and oil cellar in stainless steel vats. (Before the Second World War, the oil was stored in 400-year-old terra-cotta amphorae, which were shattered by the bombing of Spigno Saturnia.) It is vital that the olive oil be kept at a constant temperature (around 59°F) in a stable environment. In fact, the conditions for storing olive oil are not unlike those for storing wine: A dark, cool environment is best. The similarities between olive oil and wine don't end there, however. In Italy, olive oil is taken as seriously as wine. There are "Vini e Olio" shops selling both to discerning customers. What wine goes best with a fine olive oil? Luigi believed any wine at all would be wonderful! Despite the pleading requests of his patrons, Luigi would not sell the olive oil. This is because it's too rare. The process of making the oil is complex and Luigi only imported it in 5-litre quantities at a time. The oil is still only imported as the restaurant needs it so it is always as fresh as possible.

When you are using quality oil, the simplest dishes can be made delectable. Look for the Spaghetti with Garlic, Oil and Hot Pepper recipe in the Pasta chapter. This dish was served to conductor Ricardo Muti with baccala (salt cod). Mr. Muti was so impressed that he told his friend Neville Mariner, and the next month Luigi was making his simple specialty for Mr. Mariner "just the way it was served to Ricardo Muti."

There have been many famous visitors to Toronto who have savored the food at La Fenice. Among them are Yo Yo Ma who likes grilled shrimp, Alfred Brandell, who loves Luigi's gnocchi, Alan Alda, a fan of fusilli and Barolo, and Jane

Luigi's family environs

Fonda, who enjoys pasta with salad. But it's the regular customers who are the heart of La Fenice and the only reason Luigi didn't move back home to his beloved Italy.

The special olive oil that La Fenice imports is not the only "secret ingredient" in the kitchen. Also brought in, in very small quantities, is goat cheese from Spigno Saturnia. This cheese is purchased from an old friend who lives just up the hill from Luigi's childhood home. The cheese is not for sale unless you are on the good side of the farmer. Make him angry and the cheese is off-limits! He has been known to turn people back down the hill and refuse to sell cheese to them for years. Fortunately, Luigi kept relations friendly and thus was able to purchase the fresh goat cheese that is "like velvet, or silk, in the mouth" and still tastes slightly of grass. The goat cheese is delicious fresh, but to fully enjoy it you must taste it after it has been dried, salted and aged. Then the "maturo" cheese, aged properly, attains a ripe and rich flavor that is stronger than Gorgonzola – not for everyone, but heaven for afficionados.

Although most ingredients that are found in Italy can also be located in grocery or specialty stores in Canada, the crucial difference is freshness. In Italy, one buys Mozzarella di Bufala twice each day – for lunch and again for dinnner – to ensure absolute freshness.

Nothing demonstrates Luigi's appreciation for the freshest ingredients better than his birthday menu. When Luigi went home to Italy for his birthday every year, he celebrated with close friends, enjoying a dinner that was elegant in its simplicity. They ate homemade whole wheat pasta with fresh black truffles and butter. "Just truffles and butter, that's all we need." There was also a tomato salad with rughetta, (a green from the arugula family) brought straight from the garden to the birthday feast. And to finish? They could have indulged in one of Alessandra's amazing cakes, but local fruit was the choice, whatever was freshest, of course! This is the food philosophy that customers at La Fenice enjoy. Simplicity, freshness and good taste are the only requirements for a superb meal.

The recipes that follow depend on the freshest of ingredients and the highest-quality products. When you begin with the richest tomatoes (San Marzano, canned Italian tomatoes) the freshest garlic and herbs, the best cut of meat, the freshest and firmest fish and the king of Parmesan cheese, Parmigiano Reggiano, you cannot fail to create a great taste. Luigi also recommended his favorite dried pasta, Rustichella D'Abruzzo.

San Marzano tomatoes are grown in fertile soil enriched for centuries by Mount Vesuvius on the Sorrento peninsula, which divides the Gulf of Naples from the Gulf of Salerno, and where the sun shines for ten months a year. These Neapolitan tomatoes are acknowledged by experts as the best in the world. Although fresh are the best, not everyone can spend a summer in Italy. Fortunately, they are available canned in specialty shops around the world.

While you cannot buy the special olive oil that Luigi imports from his home town, he recommends an extra virgin olive oil from Liguria, the Italian Riviera, called FratelliCarli's Olio Carli, which can be purchased at specialty shops. It is a light olive oil with an acidity lower than 0.3%.

Gaeta olives are the best choice for the recipes in this book. They date back to ancient times when they were preferred by the Romans. These olives thrive on the gravelly and well drained soil in the Gaeta area which is surrounded by mountains in the north. Thus, the olive groves are protected from frost and disease. Gaeta olives have a particular, mild taste and are the preferred olive of the great chefs of Italy today.

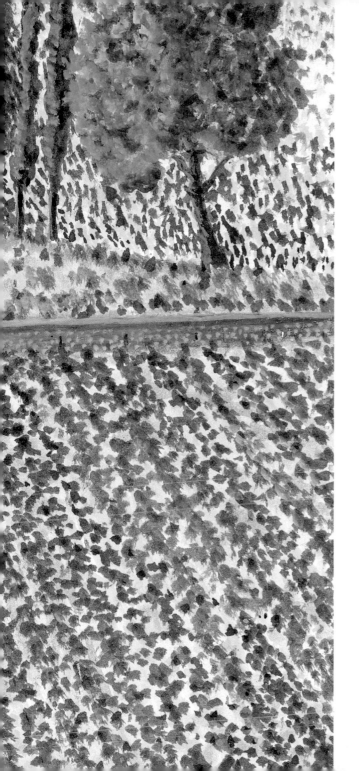

SAUCES

SALSA ALLE ACCIUGHE

ANCHOVY SAUCE

Serve with cold meats or pasta, or over steamed cauliflower.

2	hard-boiled egg yolks	2	1 Tbsp	red wine vinegar	15 mL
6	desalted anchovy fillets	6	1 Tbsp	water	15 mL
	(page 44)		1½ tsp	fresh thyme	8 mL
3 Tbsp	extra virgin olive oil	45 mL	1 Tbsp	chopped fresh Italian parsley	15 mL

∽ Place all the ingredients in a food processor and pulse for 30 seconds, then mix on high for 30 seconds.

Yield: ½ cup (125 mL)

SALSA DI FEGATINI

CHICKEN LIVER SAUCE

Serve with poultry or game such as pheasant, partridge, venison or rabbit. If this sauce is refrigerated and served cold it becomes a paté. Add green peppercorns or black truffles and serve on toast points or crackers as an hors d'oeuvre.

¼ cup	unsalted butter	50 mL	5	fresh sage leaves, chopped	5
5	whole chicken livers, coarsely chopped	5	1 Tbsp	chopped fresh rosemary	15 mL
				Salt and pepper to taste	
2	slices pancetta or bacon, coarsely chopped	2	½ cup	dry white wine	125 mL

∾ In a skillet, melt the butter over medium heat. Toss the chicken livers and pancetta, or bacon, in the melted butter until well coated. Add the herbs, salt and pepper, and saute for 3 minutes, stirring occasionally. Place the ingredients in a blender or food processor and process until very smooth. Pass the mixture through a fine colander, return it to the skillet, add the white wine and cook for 10 minutes on low heat, stirring occasionally.

∾ Serve at room temperature or just warm.

Yield: 1 cup (250 mL)

SALSA AL FINOCCHIO

FENNEL SAUCE

Serve at room temperature with a grilled or baked white fish such as sea bass, striped bass or red snapper.

2	whole fennel bulbs with green leaves	2	1 tsp	cornstarch	5 mL
¼ cup	unsalted butter	50 mL	¼ cup	dry white wine	50 mL
1	whole shallot, chopped	1	10	threads saffron	10
1 cup	fish stock (page 90)	250 mL		Juice of ½ a lemon	

~ Remove the green leaves from both fennel bulbs. Finely chop the green leaves and reserve.

~ Coarsely chop one fennel bulb and puree in a food processor. Slice the other fennel bulb.

~ Put half the butter in a skillet; add the sliced fennel and the shallot and cook for 3 minutes. Slowly add the fish stock and cook for 15 minutes. Before the liquid is completely evaporated, add the pureed fennel pulp, cornstarch, wine and saffron and cook for an additional 4 minutes. Add the remaining butter and cook for 1 minute. Add the reserved fennel leaves and mix; add the lemon juice and simmer for 2 minutes more. Serve over fish.

Yield: 1½ cups (375 mL)

SALSA VERDE

GREEN SAUCE

This is a wonderful, general purpose sauce that can be served with appetizers such as grilled vegetables or grilled meats.

4	anchovy fillets	4	6	olives, pitted	6
¼ cup	coarsely chopped fresh Italian parsley	50 mL	2	cloves garlic	2
				Salt to taste	
¼ cup	pine nuts	50 mL	½ cup	olive oil	125 mL
2 Tbsp	capers	25 mL	½ cup	red wine vinegar	125 mL
2	hard-boiled egg yolks	2			
1	slice of bread (crusts removed) soaked in 3 Tbsp (45 mL) red wine vinegar	1			

Rinse the anchovies in cold water and drain. Put all the ingredients except the olive oil and vinegar in a food processor. Pulse a few times until mixed. With the motor running, slowly pour in the oil and the vinegar. Pulse a few times until thick and creamy. The sauce can be served immediately, but the flavors improve if it rests for at least 2 hours.

NOTE: *Use your own taste to determine the ratio of olive oil to wine vinegar. You may prefer a more or less acidic flavor.*

Yield: 1½ cups (375 mL)

SALSA ALLA MENTA PER ARROSTO D'AGNELLO

MINT SAUCE FOR ROASTED LAMB

This is the perfect sauce for hot or cold roast lamb.

8	fresh mint leaves	8	2 Tbsp	white wine vinegar	25 mL
1 cup	chicken or beef broth, preferably homemade	250 mL	1½ tsp	granulated sugar	8 mL
				Pinch of salt	

∾ Place all the ingredients in a food processor and process for 30 seconds. Serve immediately.

Yield: 1¼ cups (285 mL)

SALSA ROSATA

RED SAUCE FOR CREPES STUFFED WITH RICOTTA AND SPINACH

Serve Salsa Rosata with Ricotta and Spinach Crepes (page 56) or pasta. This sauce is reminiscent of the one Luigi served with his famous agnolotti. Just add 3 ounces (75mL) of gorgozola cheese with the cream and the butter. You can use any frozen stuffed pasta for this recipe.

¼ cup	extra virgin olive oil	50 mL	6	fresh sage leaves	6
6	cloves garlic, sliced	6		Salt	
8–10	fresh or canned tomatoes	8–10	½ cup	whipping cream (35%)	125 mL
16	fresh basil leaves	16	2 Tbsp	unsalted butter	25 mL

In a large skillet heat the olive oil and saute the garlic until it is light brown. Add the tomatoes, basil, sage leaves and salt and cook for 4 minutes, if using fresh tomatoes, 10 minutes or longer if using canned tomatoes, or until the oil separates from the tomato. Add the cream and the butter and continue cooking until the sauce is warm and slightly thickened.

Yield: 3 cups (750 mL)

SALSA AL VINO ROSSO

RED WINE SAUCE

Serve with grilled or roasted beef, lamb or pork.

1 Tbsp	unsalted butter	15 mL	1 Tbsp	flour	15 mL
5	medium carrots, sliced	5	½ tsp	salt	2 mL
5	whole shallots, peeled	5	¼ tsp	pepper	1 mL
1	clove garlic, peeled	1	2¼ cups	dry red wine	500 mL
1½ tsp	chopped fresh thyme	8 mL	1½ tsp	softened butter	8 mL
4	bay leaves	4	1½ tsp	flour	8 mL

~ Melt the butter in a skillet over medium heat and saute the carrots, shallots and garlic until softened. Add the thyme and bay leaves and continue to cook for 5 minutes. Add 1 Tbsp (15 mL) flour, salt and pepper; mix well and cook until the vegetables are golden (about 10 minutes). Add the wine and simmer slowly for 1 hour.

~ Remove the sauce from the heat, remove the bay leaves and cool. Pour the sauce into a food processor and process on high for 30 seconds. Return the ingredients to the skillet and reheat until just simmering. Combine the butter with 1½ tsp (8 mL) of flour and stir the mixture into the wine sauce. Cook the sauce to desired thickness and serve.

Yield: 2 cups (500 mL)

SALSA ALLA PANNA

SAUCE WITH CREAM

This is a delicious sauce served with cold meats. To serve with a fresh salmon, hot or cold, substitute fish stock for chicken stock and fresh dill for the aromatic herbs.

FOR THE BOUQUET GARNI					
2	sprigs fresh Italian parsley	2	¼ cup	unsalted butter	50 mL
1	sprig fresh thyme	1	2 Tbsp	flour	25 mL
2	bay leaves	2	1 cup	chicken stock, preferably homemade	250 mL
7	fresh sage leaves or 1 sprig	7	1 cup	whipping cream (35%)	250 mL
1	sprig fresh rosemary	1	1	green onion, chopped	1
1	egg yolk	1			
	Salt				

⁓ First, combine the bouquet garni ingredients in a piece of cheesecloth, then tie the cloth closed.

⁓ In the top of a double boiler, melt the butter over simmering water. Add the flour and cook 1 minute. Stir in the stock and cream. Add the green onion and the bouquet garni and cook for 20 minutes. Strain and cool slightly. Add the egg yolk and beat until the yolk is completely amalgamated. Add salt to taste. If necessary, put the sauce back over simmering water until thick. Keep warm until needed.

Yield: 2 cups (500 mL)

SALSA PER PESCE ROSSO

SAUCE FOR RED FISH

Serve with panfried or grilled sardines, fresh anchovies, or other fresh oily fish such as mackerel or salmon.

1 cup	homemade mayonnaise (page 96) or prepared mayonnaise (see Note)	250 mL	1 Tbsp	finely chopped fresh Italian parsley	15 mL
			1 tsp	chopped fresh mint	5 mL
1 Tbsp	capers, unsalted, drained	15 mL	2 Tbsp	chopped fresh dill	25 mL
3 Tbsp	grappa, non-aromatic	45 mL	1 tsp	green peppercorns, drained	5 mL
	Pinch of salt				

∼ Mix all the ingredients in a blender. Let rest for 1 hour to allow flavors to mingle.

NOTE: *If using prepared mayonnaise, use ½ cup (125 mL) with 6 Tbsp (75 mL) extra virgin olive oil.*

Yield: 1 cup (250 mL)

SALSA TONNATA

TUNA SAUCE

Serve with cold meats, especially veal.

1 cup	homemade mayonnaise	250 mL	3½ oz	tuna, canned in water, drained	100 g
	(page 96) or prepared mayonnaise			Pinch of salt	
3 Tbsp	capers, unsalted and drained	45 mL	2 Tbsp	brandy or Cognac	25 mL

⌒ Blend the ingredients in a blender or food processor until smooth. Serve immediately.

Yield: 1½ cups (375 mL)

SALSA ALLE NOCI

WALNUT SAUCE

This sauce can be used to dress gnocchi, fettuccine or lasagne. Because it's so rich it is best served as an appetizer.

½ cup	walnut pieces	125 mL	2 Tbsp	chopped fresh Italian parsley	25 mL
¼ cup	pine nuts	50 mL		Salt	
2 Tbsp	extra virgin olive oil	25 mL			

⌒ In a food processor, finely chop the nuts. Heat the oil over medium-high heat and saute the nuts and parsley, stirring constantly, for 3 minutes. Toss with pasta and serve immediately. Add salt to taste. If necessary, add a little olive oil to thin the consistency.

Yield: I cup (250 mL)

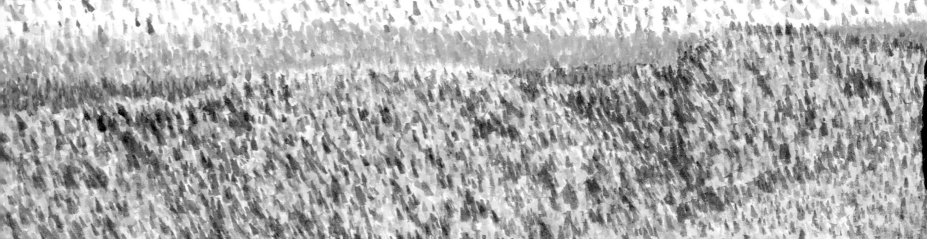

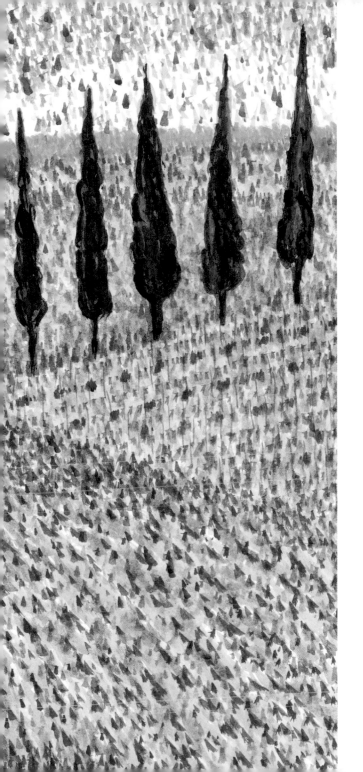

SOUPS

ZUPPA DI PESCE DEL GOLFO DI GAETA

FISH SOUP FROM THE GULF OF GAETA

If you have never eaten rockfish, you are in for a pleasant surprise. It is a red-skinned, delicate white fish with a subtle, delicious taste.

¼ cup	extra virgin olive oil	50 mL	4	sprigs fresh Italian parsley	4
8	cloves garlic, peeled and crushed	8	4	bay leaves	4
11 oz	monkfish, cut into 6, 1-inch (2.5 cm) pieces	300 g		Salt and pepper	
			2¼ lbs	rockfish	1 kg
11 oz	large scampis	300 g	11 oz	skate, skin removed, cut into 2-inch (5 cm) pieces	300 g
1 cup	white wine	250 mL			
6	tomatoes, peeled, seeded and coarsely chopped	6	1 lb	morey eel, cut into 6, 2-inch (5 cm) pieces (see Note)	500 g
6 cups	fish stock, preferably homemade (page 90)	1.5 L	6	crostini (page 39)	6
1	rib celery, with leaves, crushed	1		chopped parsley	

RECOMMENDED WINE

White. Verdicchio Castelli di Jesi Vinimar (Marche), Verdicchio, Cuprese (Marche) or Greco di Tufo (Campania)

In a large pot, heat the olive oil and brown the garlic. Add the monkfish and scampi and saute for a few minutes, stirring continually until the fish is white. Add the wine and stir until it is reduced by three-quarters. Add the tomatoes and saute for 3 minutes. Add the fish stock, celery, parsley, bay leaves, salt and pepper. Bring to a boil and cook for 8 to 10 minutes. Add the rockfish, skate and eel. Cook for 5 more minutes.

To serve, pour into a flat deep dish (to avoid breaking up the fish), or into individual bowls, and serve topped with crostini and sprinkled with chopped parsley.

NOTE: *Morey eel may need to be ordered in advance.*

Serves 6

ZUPPA AI PORRI

LEEK SOUP

½ cup	unsalted butter, divided	125 mL		Salt	
4	leeks, white part only, finely chopped	4	2 Tbsp	whipping cream (35%)	25 mL
			1 Tbsp	chopped fresh Italian parsley	15 mL
8 cups	chicken stock, preferably homemade	2 L		Freshly grated Parmigiano Reggiano cheese	
¾ lb	potatoes, preferably Yukon Gold, peeled and thinly sliced	340 g	30	small slices white bread, toasted	30

In a large saucepan, melt half the butter and saute the leeks until they are transparent. Add 2 cups (500 mL) stock and bring to a boil. Cook the leeks until they are soft. Add the remaining stock and return to a boil. Add the potatoes and cook over moderate heat for about 20 minutes. Salt to taste. Just before serving, add the remaining butter, cream and parsley. Return to a boil and remove when the soup is heated through.

Serve topped with grated Parmesan cheese and toasted bread on the side.

Serves 6

PASSATELLI DI PATATE IN BRODO

LITTLE POTATO DUMPLINGS IN BROTH

6	medium potatoes	6L		Pinch of nutmeg	
2 Tbsp	unsalted butter	25 mL		Salt	
2 Tbsp	Parmigiano Reggiano cheese,	25 mL	⅓ cup	flour	75 mL
	plus extra for serving		1 cup	vegetable oil	250 mL
3	egg yolks	3	6 cups	beef or chicken stock,	1.5 L
2 Tbsp	chopped fresh Italian parsley	25 mL		preferably homemade	

RECOMMENDED WINE

White. Frascati (Lazio)

Chardonnay, Lungarotti
(Umbria)

Chardonnay, Valdadige,
Armani (Trentino-Alto Adige)

∼ Boil the potatoes with the skins on until tender. Peel the potatoes and pass them through a potato ricer. Stir in the butter, cheese, egg yolks, parsley, nutmeg and salt to taste. Mix well.

∼ Form into small balls and dredge in flour. Heat the vegetable oil and the stock in separate pots. Fry the passatelli in the hot vegetable oil until golden. Drain on paper towels and serve in hot stock with Parmigiano Reggiano cheese.

Serves 6

PASTA E FAGIOLI

PASTA WITH BEANS

A unique approach to breaking up canned tomatoes is to squeeze them by hand. This creates a "filetto di pomodoro" and is much more effective than chopping the tomatoes.

FOR THE BEANS

1 lb	white navy beans	500 g
2	cloves garlic, peeled and crushed	2
1	rib celery, crushed	1
1	bunch fresh basil	1
2 Tbsp	olive oil	25 mL
	Salt to taste	

FOR THE PASTA

1	large onion, chopped	1
⅓ cup	extra virgin olive oil	75 mL
1 tsp	dried chili peppers (optional)	5 mL
2	28 oz cans tomatoes, broken up	2
5 cups	water	1.25 L
10	fresh basil leaves	10
1	rib celery, crushed	1
	Salt and pepper	
½ lb	tubettini or ditali pasta	250 g
	Grated Parmigiano Reggiano cheese	

～ Place the dried beans in a pot and add enough cold water to cover them by 4 inches (10 cm). Add the garlic, celery, basil, olive oil and salt. Bring to a boil, reduce heat and simmer the beans for about 1 hour until cooked but not dry. Add hot water as needed to keep the beans covered. Remove the basil and celery. Set the beans aside.

～ In a large pot, saute the onion in olive oil until light brown. Add the chili peppers, if using, and the tomatoes. Cook uncovered over medium heat for 30 minutes. Add the water, basil, celery, salt and pepper to taste and bring to a boil. Add the beans with their liquid and cook for 25 minutes over medium heat. Add the dried pasta and cook al dente. Add water as needed to create a soup (not too thick). Add salt and pepper to taste. Remove the basil and celery and serve topped with Parmigiano Reggiano.

Serves 12

RECOMMENDED WINE
Red. Merlot "Collio", Venica & Venica (Friuli-Venezia Giulia) Schioppettino, G. Dorigo (Friuli-Venezia Giulia)

PASTA CON LENTICCHIE

PASTA WITH LENTILS

FOR THE LENTILS			FOR THE PASTA		
1 cup	green lentils, washed and sorted for stones	250 g	1 Tbsp	olive oil	15 mL
⅓ lb	salt pork or pancetta	150 g	1	onion, finely chopped	1
1	whole small onion, peeled	1	6	tomatoes, peeled, seeded and chopped	6
1	fresh tomato, cut in half	1	4 cups	water	1 L
2	cloves garlic, peeled and crushed	2		salt	
1	rib celery, crushed	1	1	sprig fresh basil	1
1	sprig fresh basil	1	1	rib celery, crushed	1
¼ cup	olive oil	50 mL	¾ lb	tubetti	375 g
				Grated Parmigiano Reggiano cheese	
				Pepper	

RECOMMENDED WINE
Red. Merlot (Friuli-Venezia Giulia) or Barbera D'Alba (Piemonte)

~ Place the lentils, pork or pancetta, onion, tomato, garlic, celery, basil and olive oil in a large pot and cover with salted water. Bring to a boil and cook uncovered on low heat for 1 hour. Add extra water if needed. Remove the vegetables, herbs and salt pork, or pancetta, with a slotted spoon and discard. Set the lentils aside.

~ In another deep pot, heat the olive oil and saute the onion until transparent. Add the tomatoes and cook for 10 minutes, then add the water, salt, basil and celery. When the vegetables and herbs are cooked, add the lentils. Bring to a boil and cook for 15 minutes. Remove the celery and basil. Add the pasta (make sure there is enough liquid for the broth; add more water if necessary). When the pasta is cooked al dente, remove the pot from the stove and serve. Top with grated Parmigiano Reggiano and pepper to taste.

Serves 8

BRODETTO DI FAGIANO

PHEASANT BROTH

For a delicious change from chicken soup, try pheasant.

1	pheasant, cleaned	1	1	fresh tomato, cut in 4 pieces	1
2	carrots, coarsely chopped	2		Salt	
1	rib celery, crushed	1			

~ Place the pheasant in a stockpot and barely cover with cold water. Add the remaining ingredients and bring to a boil. Reduce to a simmer, cover and cook slowly for 1½ hours. Remove the cover and continue to cook for another half hour.

~ Remove the solids and strain. Cool. Refrigerate overnight. Skim off the fat (there will not be a lot). Reheat and serve.

Serves 6

PUREA DI ZUCCA

PUREE OF SQUASH SOUP

½ cup	olive oil	125 mL	1	bouquet garni, consisting of:	1
1	white onion, peeled and chopped	1		1 sprig fresh basil, 4 bay leaves,	
2	ribs celery, no leaves, crushed	2		4 fresh mint leaves, 1 small white	
2 lbs	butternut squash, peeled and cut	1 kg		turnip (tied in cheesecloth)	
	into small pieces			Salt	
4	medium potatoes, preferably	4	½ cup	whipping cream (35%)	125 mL
	Yukon Gold, peeled and diced		6	slices toasted bread	6
6¾ cups	chicken stock, preferably	1.5 L	1 Tbsp	unsalted butter	15 mL
	homemade (or water)			Pepper	
1	heel of Parmesan cheese, rind	1			
	well scraped				

RECOMMENDED WINE
White. Vernaccia di San Gimignano (Toscana)

∽ In a deep pot, heat the olive oil and saute the onion until it is transparent. Add the celery and saute for 2 minutes. Add the squash, potatoes, stock, Parmesan and bouquet garni tied with a string to the handle of the pot. Cook over medium heat until the potatoes and squash are soft. Remove the celery, Parmesan and bouquet garni. Place the remaining contents in a food processor and puree.

∽ Return contents to the pan, bring to a boil and cook for 1 minute, then add salt to taste. Remove the soup from the heat and add the cream. Mix well and serve with the toasted bread on the side, spread with some of the butter and topped with pepper.

Serves 6

ZUPPA DI BACCALA CON PATATE

SOUP WITH SALT COD AND POTATOES

2¼ lbs	baccala (salt cod)	1 kg	4 cups	water	1 L
½ cup	extra virgin olive oil	125 mL	3	medium potatoes, preferably	3
1	medium onion, thinly sliced or chopped	1		Yukon Gold, peeled and diced Salt and pepper	
6	medium fresh, ripe tomatoes, thinly sliced	6		Chopped fresh Italian parsley	
10	fresh basil leaves	10	8	crostini (toasted Italian bread, preferably sourdough, rubbed	8
4	bay leaves	4		with peeled garlic and sprinkled	
1	rib celery, coarsely chopped	1		with extra virgin olive oil).	

Cut the cod into 3-inch (7.5 cm) pieces and place in cold water for 3 days, changing the water daily. When ready to use, drain the cod, rinse and pat dry.

In a 4-inch (10 cm) deep pot, heat the olive oil and saute the onion until transparent. Add the tomatoes and saute for 5 minutes then add the herbs and celery. Add the water and boil for 5 minutes. Add the potatoes. When the potatoes are partially cooked (about 10 minutes) add the cod, salt and pepper to taste and cook, uncovered, for another 15 minutes.

Place the soup in a large tureen or in individual bowls. Sprinkle the soup with chopped parsley and pass the crostini.

Serves 4

MENU SUGGESTION
If serving the soup as a main course, start with Grilled Shrimp, Calamari Stuffed and Grilled, or Calamari Stuffed with Monkfish.

RECOMMENDED WINE
Light Red. Aglianico del Vulture (Basilicata)

FRASCARELLI ALL'UOVO

SOUP MADE WITH A BRANCH OF A BUSH

This recipe is fun. It is a medieval, primitive, creative recipe, which was made in the countryside when times were tough, and when there were no tools. Today in Italy this recipe is made commercially. Try it with the Pheasant Broth.

3	eggs	3	10 cups	chicken stock, preferably	2.5 L
¼ cup	water	50 mL		homemade	
2 cups	flour	500 mL		grated Parmigiano Reggiano cheese	
	Pinch of salt				
1	dried branch of any bush stripped of its leaves, or a small, clean, vegetable brush	1			

~ Beat the eggs until combined and add the water to obtain a liquid consistency. On a flat surface, spread 1 cup (250 mL) flour very thinly. Wet the branch or brush in the egg mixture and shake the egg droplets over the flour. Sweep the flour and egg droplets into a fine sieve and sift the excess flour onto the flat surface. Repeat, using all the egg mixture and the flour. Place the frascarelli on a clean cloth to dry until ready to cook.

~ Bring a pot of water to a boil and add the frascarelli. Cook until the pasta rises to the surface (a few minutes). Strain. In a separate pot, bring the chicken stock to a boil, add the cooked pasta and serve immediately with grated Parmigiano Reggiano.

NOTE: *By cooking the pasta separately the full flavor of the chicken stock will be retained; otherwise, the flour from the pasta will deplete the stock of some of its flavor.*

Serves 6

MINESTRA DI RISO ALLA VENETA

VENETIAN SOUP WITH RICE

This is a delicious hearty soup, a meal in itself.

1¼ lbs	sweet Italian sausage	600 g	8 cups	chicken stock, preferably	2 L
1 Tbsp	olive oil	15 mL		homemade	
1 cup	rapini	250 mL	1 cup	Arborio rice, washed	250 mL
½ lb	lean pork, minced	250 g	4 Tbsp	chopped fresh Italian parsley	50 mL
1	medium onion, chopped	1	3 Tbsp	grated Parmigiano Reggiano	45 mL
4 Tbsp plus	unsalted butter	50 mL		cheese	
2 tsp		10 mL		Salt and pepper	

In a skillet, boil the whole sausage in about ½ inch (1 cm) of water for 10 minutes. Discard the water then cut the sausage into bite-sized pieces. Heat the olive oil and lightly brown the sausage pieces. Remove and set aside.

Clean and remove the bitter stalks from the rapini. Boil the rapini until just cooked then drain and chop it finely.

In a large saucepan, brown the pork with the onion in 2 tsp (10 mL) butter. Add the sausage, rapini and 2 cups (500 mL) of the stock. Add the remaining stock a little at a time until it is all incorporated. Bring to a boil, add the rice and cook for 15 minutes. Stir in the remaining butter, parsley, Parmesan, salt and pepper to taste. Mix well and serve immediately. If desired, serve additional Parmesan on the side.

Serves 6

RECOMMENDED WINE
White. Soave, Bolla (Veneto)

APPETIZERS AND FIRST COURSES

ACCIUGHE DISALATE

DESALTED ANCHOVIES

These can be added to a plate of antipasti.

30	whole, salted anchovies	30	2 Tbsp	extra virgin olive oil	25 mL
½ cup	red wine vinegar	125 mL	1 Tbsp	chopped fresh Italian parsley	15 mL
	Juice of 1 lemon		4	lemon wedges	4
1 Tbsp	capers	15 mL			

RECOMMENDED WINE
White. Verdicchio, Marchetti (Marche)

〜 Place the anchovies in a deep dish with half the vinegar and half the lemon juice. Stir the anchovies in the liquid to remove the salt. Remove the anchovies and discard the liquid. Repeat the process with the remaining vinegar and lemon juice. Remove the anchovies and rinse under cold water. Pat dry.

〜 Place the anchovies on a serving dish, flat or rolled with a caper inside. If they're left flat, sprinkle with some capers. Sprinkle with extra virgin olive oil, chopped parsley and add a wedge of lemon.

Serves 4

ALICI FRESCHE, OREGANATE

ANCHOVIES WITH THE SCENT OF OREGANO

2¼ lbs	fresh anchovies	1 kg	1 Tbsp	chopped fresh oregano, or	15 mL
6 Tbsp	extra virgin olive oil	75 mL		2 tsp (8 mL) dried	
12	bay leaves	12	3	cloves garlic, thinly sliced	3
¾ cup	fine breadcrumbs	175 mL	⅓ cup	red wine vinegar	75mL
2 Tbsp	chopped fresh Italian parsley	25 mL		Salt and pepper	
1 Tbsp	chopped fresh mint	15 mL			

∽ Preheat a broiler to 450°F (230°C).

∽ To clean the anchovies, gut them, remove the heads, then rinse the anchovies in cold water and dry on paper towels. In an 8 x 10-inch (20 x 25 cm) deep oven dish, heat half the olive oil, making sure to distribute the oil over the bottom and up the sides. Place 4 bay leaves on the bottom of the dish and sprinkle with ⅓ of the breadcrumbs; line with ⅓ of the anchovies and sprinkle with some of the breadcrumbs, herbs, garlic, olive oil, vinegar, salt and pepper. Top with 4 bay leaves. Repeat, making 3 layers. Broil until the top is golden. Serve.

Serves 4

MENU SUGGESTION
Serve as an appetizer or for lunch with a salad of Boston lettuce.

RECOMMENDED WINE
Red. Chianti Classico (Toscana)
White. Pinot Grigio (Friuli-Venezia Giulia)

CARCIOFI IN PASTELLA

ARTICHOKES IN BATTER

These delicious artichokes can be served as a first course or as an appetizer with drinks.

4	medium artichokes	4			Salt	
2	eggs, separated	2	2 cups	peanut oil	500 mL
1 cup	flour	250 g	8	fresh mint leaves, finely chopped	8
½ cup	white wine	125 mL	2	lemons	2

RECOMMENDED WINE

White. Gewurztraminer, Alois Lageder (Trentino-Alto Adige) Greco di Tufo, Mastroberardino (Campania)

~ Clean each artichoke by cutting off the stem at the base and removing the outer leaves until the core becomes visible (the leaves will be pale green and a cone shape will emerge). Cut ⅓ off the top of the cone. Cut the artichoke in half vertically. With a small, sharp knife, cut away the fuzzy choke. From the outside of the artichoke heart, pare away any remaining tough green parts. Place the artichoke heart in water with lemon juice to avoid discoloration. Repeat with remaining artichokes.

~ In a mixing bowl, beat the egg yolks, add the flour, white wine and a pinch of salt. Add a little water if the batter is too thick. Beat the egg whites until stiff and fold into the batter.

~ Drain the artichokes and pat dry. Dip the artichokes in the batter to coat.

~ In a deep skillet, heat the oil and when it's very hot add the artichokes. Fry for about 2 minutes, or until they are golden brown and crisp. Place artichokes on absorbent paper to drain. Serve hot with chopped mint on top and lemon wedges on the side.

Serves 4

TORTA DI CARCIOFI

ARTICHOKE TART

1 cup	flour	250 mL	2 Tbsp	chopped fresh Italian parsley	25 mL
	Salt and pepper to taste		2	eggs, beaten	2
½ cup	unsalted butter, cold	125 mL	2 Tbsp	grated Parmigiano Reggiano	25 mL
1½ cups	fresh ricotta cheese	375 mL		cheese	
7	medium artichokes	7	1	egg white, beaten with 1 Tbsp	1
	Juice of 1 lemon			(15 mL) water	
2 Tbsp	extra virgin olive oil	25 mL			

〜 Preheat an oven to 375°F (190°C).

〜 In a food processor, combine the flour with a pinch of salt. Cut in the butter then add half the ricotta cheese. Process until the dough forms a ball. Add a pinch of salt. Wrap and rest the pastry in a cool place for 1 hour.

〜 Clean the artichokes (page 46). Thinly slice the artichoke hearts and place them in cold water with the lemon juice. Drain when ready to use. Pat dry.

〜 Heat the olive oil in a skillet and saute the sliced artichokes with the parsley and 2 Tbsp (25 mL) water. Cook for 15 minutes or until al dente, adding more water if necessary. Place the artichokes in a mixing bowl with the eggs and the remaining ricotta, Parmesan, salt and pepper.

〜 On a floured surface, roll out half the dough and place it in a buttered 10-inch (25 cm) pie plate. Pour in the artichoke mixture and top with the remaining dough; crimp the edges. Brush with the egg white.

〜 Bake the tart for 35 minutes. Test for doneness. The crust should be golden brown. Serve hot or cold.

NOTE: *As an alternative, breadcrumbs can be substituted for the pastry. Butter a casserole dish; spread a layer of breadcrumbs on the bottom, top with the artichoke mixture, finish with a mixture of breadcrumbs and Parmesan cheese, and dot with butter. Bake at 400°F (200°C) for 20 minutes or until the top is brown. Just before serving, sprinkle with fresh lemon juice.*

Serves 8

RECOMMENDED WINE
White. Greco di Tufo, Mastroberardino (Campania) Gewurztraminer, Alois Lageder (Trentino-Alto Adige)

CARCIOFI DI FONDI-ALL' ERBE SELVATICHE

ARTICHOKES WITH WILD HERBS FROM THE COUNTRYSIDE

This artichoke recipe is a specialty of the Gulf of Gaeta. Luigi won an award for his delicious interpretation of this regional favorite.

2 cups	fresh breadcrumbs	500 mL		Salt and pepper	
3 Tbsp	chopped fresh dill	45 mL	6	medium artichokes	6
3 Tbsp	chopped fresh mint	45 mL	6	fresh mint leaves	6
2	garlic cloves, finely chopped	2	6	sprigs fresh dill	6
½ cup	extra virgin olive oil	125 mL			

MENU SUGGESTION
Artichokes are so mild that this dish goes well with almost anything. Some good choices are poached fish, salmon or fresh cod.

RECOMMENDED WINE
White. Gewurztraminer, Alois Lageder (Trentino-Alto Adige)

~ Combine the breadcrumbs with the first two herbs, the garlic and half the oil in a food processor or blender.

~ Prepare the artichokes: Trim the stems at the bottom of the artichokes so that they are flat and stand straight up. Cut about 1 inch (2.5 cm) off the tips of the artichokes and remove some of the hard outer leaves so that just the heart of the artichoke is exposed. Gradually open the core of the artichoke, without breaking the leaves; rinse the artichokes, sprinkle with salt and pepper and stuff the cavity with the prepared mixture.

~ Place the prepared artichokes in a shallow pan and pour approximately 1½ inches (3.75 cm) of salted water around them (just enough water to steam). Scatter mint leaves, sprigs of dill and the remaining olive oil over the artichokes and cover. Steam artichokes on top of the stove for 20–25 minutes, or in the oven at 450°F (230°C).

~ Place the artichokes in a serving dish and pour the cooking liquid around them. Open the artichokes and serve.

Serves 6

CIPOLLE AL FORNO

BAKED ONIONS

My husband and I wandered into a local bakery shop in the market area of Catania, Sicily, where we were drawn by an incredibly delicious smell. On top of the counter sat a tray of several prepared yummies, including roasted peppers and sweet baked onions. We purchased some of everything and set out a board of appetizers with a loaf of warm, fresh bread from the bakery. The onions were sweet and perfectly cooked. I asked Luigi to reproduce them.

6	medium white bulb onions, or red onions	6		Salt and pepper	
			2 Tbsp	chopped fresh Italian parsley	25 mL
3 Tbsp	extra virgin olive oil	45 mL			

∾ Preheat an oven to 350°F (180°C).

∾ Remove the skin from the onions. Blanch the onions in boiling water for 6 minutes. Drain and cut the onions in half horizontally. Smear the bottom of a baking dish with 1 Tbsp (15 mL) olive oil. Place the onions in the dish cut side up and sprinkle with the remaining olive oil, salt and pepper and parsley. Bake for 1 hour.

Serves 6

MENU SUGGESTION
Serve the onions as part of an antipasto plate or with meats.

RECOMMEDED WINE
Red. Valpolicello, Classico (Toscana)

CALAMARI FARCITI, GRATINATI

CALAMARI STUFFED AND BROILED

Another delicious specialty of the Gulf of Gaeta, this makes a perfect appetizer with a glass of white wine.

8	slices bread	8	2½ Tbsp	fresh Italian parsley	30 mL
2	cloves garlic	2		Salt and pepper	
½ cup	extra virgin olive oil	125 mL	6	calamari, small-to-medium, cleaned	6
¼ cup	red wine vinegar	50 mL	12	bay leaves	12

MENU SUGGESTION
*Serve with a second plate of
fresh fish, Linguini from
Formia, Linguini in Light
Lobster Sauce, or Risotto with
Seafood. If serving the calamari
as a main dish, serve with
a salad.*

RECOMMENED WINE
*White. Fiano di Avellino,
Mastroberardino (Campania)
or Verdicchio (Marche)*

~ Preheat a broiler.

~ In a food processor, blend the bread, garlic, half the olive oil, half the wine vinegar, the parsley, salt and pepper.

~ Open the calamari; cut down one side and open to a butterfly (retain the tentacles for later). Place on a flat surface with the skin side down and with a sharp knife make a diagonal cut on the inside of the calamari without cutting through it.

~ Cook the calamari in a pot of boiling water just until they curl. Remove the calamari immediately, fill with the bread stuffing (reserving some of the stuffing for later) and fold. The diagonal cut will now be on the outside.

~ Put 6 bay leaves with the remaining olive oil and wine vinegar in the bottom of an ovenproof dish. Place the calamari on top of the bay leaves and place one bay leaf on top of each calamari. Top with the remaining stuffing and broil until the bread mixture is golden. The tentacles can be placed in the same dish topped with some of the stuffing. Serve the calamari whole.

Serves 3

CALAMARI FARCITI CON PESCATRICE

CALAMARI STUFFED WITH MONKFISH

2 lbs	12 small calamari, cleaned	1 kg	3 Tbsp	finely chopped garlic	45 mL
⅓ lb	fresh monkfish	150 g	4 Tbsp plus	chopped fresh Italian	50 mL plus
½ cup	flour	125 mL	1 Tbsp	parsley	15 mL
½ cup	unsalted butter	125 mL	4	fresh basil leaves, chopped	4
½ cup plus	extra virgin olive oil	125 mL plus	¾ cup	dry white wine	175 mL
2 Tbsp		25 mL	10	drops Worcestershire sauce	10
1	small onion, finely chopped	1	¼ cup	balsamic vinegar	50 mL

Rinse the calamari well in cold water, making sure all the insides have been removed. Dip the calamari in boiling water for fifteen seconds, remove, cool and set aside.

Dice the monkfish and toss it in flour. In a saucepan, melt the butter with 7 Tbsp (105 mL) olive oil and saute the onion, garlic, parsley, basil and monkfish for about 3 minutes. Add ½ cup (125 mL) of the wine and cook, covered, over medium heat until it has evaporated (about 10 minutes). Add the Worcestershire sauce and mix.

Stuff the calamari with the monkfish mixture and close the tops with toothpicks. Brush the calamari with 1 Tbsp (15 mL) olive oil, and, in a cast iron skillet over medium heat, cook the calamari with the remaining ¼ cup (50 mL) wine for about 5 minutes. Meanwhile, combine 2 Tbsp (25 mL) olive oil with the balsamic vinegar and 1 Tbsp (15 mL) parsley. Remove the calamari to a hot serving plate and top with the dressing.

Serves 4

MENU SUGGESTION
For a second course, serve Spaghettini with Clam Sauce.

RECOMMENDED WINE
White. Pinot Grigio, Armani (Trentino-Alto-Adige), Falerio dei Colli Ascolani, Saladini Pilastri (Marche)

CARPACCIO DI MANZO ALL'EMILIANA

THINLY SLICED RAW BEEF

1 lb	beef tenderloin or eye of round	500 g	1 Tbsp	capers	15 mL
1	lemon	1	4	sprigs fresh Italian parsley	4
	Salt		6 ounces	Parmigiano Reggiano cheese	175 g
4 Tbsp	extra virgin olive oil	50 mL			

⌇ Roll the meat tightly in plastic wrap and place in the freezer until it has just hardened (not frozen) for about 2 hours. This makes it possible to slice the meat thinly.

⌇ Remove the meat from the freezer and slice it very thinly. Flatten the slices with the flat side of a large knife. Put the slices on a flat, cold plate and sprinkle with the juice of ¼ of the lemon. Sprinkle with salt and olive oil; top with capers. Thickly slice the Parmesan and place the slices on top of the meat in the center of the plate. Garnish with parsley and serve with remaining lemon, cut into wedges.

Serves 4

PANE COTTO CON FAGIOLI

COOKED BREAD WITH BEANS

Don't let the title discourage you. This is absolutely delicious and very different. In Italy, it is served for breakfast! In North America, try it for lunch with a salad.

4	cloves garlic, sliced or chopped	4	15 oz	white navy beans, cooked	450 g
½ cup	extra virgin olive oil	125 mL	12	fresh basil leaves	12
1¾ cups	fresh Italian sourdough loaf	450 mL		Salt	
	with hard crust, diced into			Dried chili peppers, or jalapeno	
	small cubes			pepper to taste	
2 cups	water	500 mL			

In a 9-inch (23 cm) skillet, saute the garlic in half the olive oil. When the garlic is brown, remove the pan from the heat, add the bread and water and bring to a boil. Add the beans, half the basil, salt and hot peppers and cook for 10 minutes. Add the remaining oil and top with the remaining fresh basil. Serve with Parmesan on the side.

Serves 6

RECOMMENDED WINE
Red. Merlot, Collio (Friuli-Venezia Giulia)

CRESPELLE FARCITE CON CARNE, GRATINATE

CREPES WITH MEAT AND WHITE SAUCE

FOR THE CREPES

3	large eggs	3
1¾ cups	whole milk	425 mL
¾ cup	flour	175 mL
3 Tbsp	olive oil	45 mL
3 Tbsp	unsalted butter, melted	45 mL

FOR THE BECHAMEL SAUCE

1½ Tbsp	unsalted butter	20 mL
¼	onion, chopped	¼
2 Tbsp	flour	25 mL
2 cups	whole milk, heated	500 mL
	Salt and pepper	
	Pinch of nutmeg	

FOR THE FILLING

¼ cup	unsalted butter	
1	carrot, very finely chopped	1
1	onion, very finely chopped	1
1	rib celery, very finely chopped	1
2 Tbsp	finely chopped fresh Italian parsley	25 mL
6	fresh basil leaves	6
¾ lb	lean ground beef	375 g
¼ cup	prosciutto, chopped	50 mL
2 Tbsp	dried porcini mushrooms, reconstituted, drained and chopped	25 mL
1 Tbsp	truffle, shaved (optional)	15 mL
	Salt and pepper	
	Pinch of nutmeg	
1 cup	dry white wine	250 mL
1 Tbsp	flour	15 mL
3	fresh tomatoes, peeled, seeded and chopped	3
1½ cups	Farmer's Ragu sauce (page 66)	375 mL
½ cup	grated Parmigiano Reggiano cheese	125 mL

MENU SUGGESTION
For a main course, serve Crown Roast of Lamb or Roasted Leg of Lamb with Herbs.

RECOMMENDED WINE
Red. Chianti; Badia a Passignano, Antinori (Toscana), Valpolicella Classico, Boscaini (Veneto)

~ Blend the ingredients with a whisk. Let the crepe batter rest in the refrigerator for at least 2 hours before using it.

~ Use an 8-inch (20 cm) crepe pan that has been treated with hot oil (see Note). Over medium-high heat, add ¼ cup (50mL) of the batter to the pan. Tilt and rotate the pan until the batter is evenly distributed. Cook the crepe for about 35 seconds or until it is brown; turn and cook the other side for about 15 seconds.

~ Remove the crepe from the pan and place it on top of a cloth that is large enough to accommodate the twelve crepes. This procedure will limit condensation so the crepes do not become soggy; they will dry quickly. When dry, the crepes can then be piled on a plate, covered with a cloth towel and stored until ready to use.

⁓ In a medium saucepan, saute the onion in the butter until it is transparent, without browning. Add the flour and stir, cooking for about 2 minutes; add the milk, a little at a time until it is well mixed with the butter, onion, flour mixture; add salt, pepper and nutmeg. Bring to a slow boil over moderate heat, stirring constantly for about 10 minutes until the sauce has thickened. Remove the sauce from the heat and cool until it is lukewarm. Pulse the bechamel sauce in a food processor for 30 seconds on low speed. When ready to use, reheat, stirring continuously with a wooden spoon.

⁓ In a large skillet, melt the butter then add the carrot, onion and celery and saute the vegetables until they are transparent. Add the parsley and basil, stir and cook for 1 minute. Add the ground beef and mix thoroughly. Cook for 3 minutes. Add the prosciutto, mushrooms and truffle, if using, salt, pepper and nutmeg. Stir well. Add the wine and reduce completely. Sprinkle the flour over the mixture and stir well. Add the tomatoes, 2 Tbsp (25 mL) of the Farmer's Ragu Sauce and pepper. Continue cooking over moderate heat. When the sauce thickens, remove it from the heat, and cool it in a bowl.

⁓ Put the prepared crepes on a flat surface, place 1½ Tbsp (20 mL) of the meat filling in each crepe and roll it up lengthwise. Use individual oven dishes or a large oven dish that will accommodate all the crepes. Butter the bottom of the oven dish and cover it with some of the bechamel sauce. Place the crepes on the bechamel sauce and top with some of the Ragu sauce, a layer of bechamel sauce, more Ragu sauce and finally Parmesan cheese. Place the dish under the broiler and broil until golden. Serve two crepes per person.

NOTE: *To treat the crepe pan, put oil in the pan and heat; discard the hot oil and wipe the pan with a paper towel.*

Serves 6

CRESPELLE DI RICOTTA CON SPINACI

CREPES WITH RICOTTA AND SPINACH

	Basic recipe for crepes (page 54)		1	whole egg	1
				Pinch of salt	
FOR THE STUFFING			1 tsp	nutmeg	5 mL
1 lb	ricotta cheese	500 g	3 Tbsp plus	grated Parmigiano	45 mL plus
2	bunches fresh spinach, cooked,	2	½ cup	Reggiano cheese	125 mL
	squeezed dry and finely chopped			Salsa Rosata (page 25)	

MENU SUGGESTION

For a main course, serve veal piccata.

RECOMMENDED WINE

Red. Chianti Classico, Badia a Passignano, Antinori (Toscano) Rubesco, Lungarotti (Umbria)

∽ Preheat an oven to 450°F (230°C).

∽ Mix the ricotta, spinach, egg, salt, nutmeg and 3 Tbsp (45 mL) Parmigiano Reggiano together.

∽ Place 1 Tbsp (15 mL) of the ricotta mixture in each crepe and roll it up lengthwise. Repeat, using all the crepes.

∽ Place the crepes in a single layer in a greased baking dish and bake until the sides start to brown, 12 to 15 minutes. Remove the crepes from the oven, serve two crepes per person and top with Salsa Rosata. Sprinkle with remaining Parmesan and serve.

Serves 6

MELENZANE AI FUNGHI

EGGPLANT WITH MUSHROOMS

2	medium eggplants	2	2	fresh tomatoes, peeled, seeded and chopped	2
1 cup	fresh porcini mushrooms, or other mushrooms	225 g	4	fresh basil leaves, chopped	4
2	cloves garlic, chopped	2		Salt and pepper	
1 Tbsp	chopped fresh Italian parsley	15 mL	½ cup	breadcrumbs	125 mL
½ cup	extra virgin olive oil	125 mL			

- Preheat a broiler.

- Cut the top stem off from the eggplant. Cut the eggplant in half lengthwise and place on a work surface. Remove the center pulp with a spoon and dice. Set aside the empty eggplant skins.

- Wipe the mushrooms with a damp paper towel and slice them thinly.

- In a skillet, saute the garlic and parsley in half the olive oil. When the garlic is golden, add the diced eggplant and the mushrooms and saute for 2 minutes. Add the tomatoes, basil, salt and pepper, and cook for 10 minutes.

- Oil the bottom of an ovenproof casserole. Fill the eggplant skins with the mushroom/eggplant mixture. Sprinkle with breadcrumbs and the remaining olive oil. Place the shells in the casserole and broil until the tops are brown. Serve hot.

Serves 4

MENU SUGGESTION
For a main course, serve Chicken with Dill or Chicken Diavolo .

RECOMMENDED WINE
Red. Duca Enrico, Duca di Salaparuta (Sicilia) Taurasi, 'Radici', Mastroberardino (Campania)

MELENZANE ALL'ORIENTALE

EGGPLANT ORIENTAL

2	medium eggplants	2	1 Tbsp	chopped fresh basil	15 mL
1	small eggplant	1	1 Tbsp	chopped fresh Italian parsley	15 mL
¾ cup	extra virgin olive oil	175 mL	4 Tbsp	fresh breadcrumbs, made	50 mL
2	cloves garlic, sliced	2		without crusts	
½	cooking onion, chopped	½		Salt and pepper	
6	fresh tomatoes or canned tomatoes, peeled, seeded, chopped and drained	6			

RECOMMENDED WINE

White. Vernaccia di San Gimignano (Toscana) Vermentino Sella & Mosca (Sardegna)

~ Preheat an oven to 350°F (180°C).

~ Peel all the eggplants and cut them lengthwise into 6 slices each.

~ Heat ½ cup (125 mL) less 2 Tbsp (25 mL) of the olive oil in a large skillet over medium heat and fry the eggplant until just golden on both sides. Drain on paper towels. Chop the smaller eggplant into tiny squares and set aside.

~ Heat ¼ cup (50 mL) olive oil and brown the garlic with the onions until they are transparent. Add the tomatoes, squeezed by hand if canned or coarsely chopped if fresh, and cook for 8 minutes. Add the small, chopped eggplant, basil, parsley, breadcrumbs, salt and pepper. Cook the mixture until slightly thickened.

~ Oil the bottom of a large ovenproof dish with the remaining 2 Tbsp (25 mL) of olive oil. Place half the eggplant slices in the dish, top with the stuffing, then with the remaining slices.

~ Sprinkle the top with a little extra virgin olive oil and bake for 30 minutes. Remove and cool. Serve at room temperature.

Serves 4–6

BACCALA ALLA BUONGUSTAIO

GOURMET SALT COD

2¼ lbs	salt cod (baccala)	1 kg		Salt and pepper	
2 cups	flour	500 mL	6–8	bay leaves	6–8
1 cup	extra virgin olive oil	250 mL	2	red peppers, roasted and cut	2
3	cloves garlic, thinly sliced	3		in strips	
½ cup	breadcrumbs	125 mL	1 Tbsp	capers	15 mL
2 Tbsp	fresh Italian parsley	25 mL	1	lemon	1

~ Preheat an oven to 450°F (230°C).

~ Place the salt cod in fresh water for 3 days before using, changing the water daily. When ready to use, drain, rinse, cut the cod into pieces and dry on paper towels. Dip the cod pieces in flour. Shake off excess flour. Heat half the oil in a pan until hot and fry the cod until brown on both sides. Remove the cod to a dish. Discard the oil and wipe the pan clean.

~ Add the remaining oil to the pan and saute the garlic. Add half the breadcrumbs and half the parsley, salt, pepper and bay leaves. Mix. Place this mixture on the bottom of a baking dish and top with the baccala. Place the remaining breadcrumbs and parsley, the red pepper strips and capers on top of the baccala and bake for 15 minutes. Remove the dish from the oven, squeeze the lemon over the cod and serve.

NOTE: *Taste before adding salt to this dish.*

Serves 4

MENU SUGGESTION
For a main course, serve a
leg of lamb and vegetables.

RECOMMENDED WINE
White. Soave (Veneto)
Red. Chianti Classico, Badia a
Passignano, Riserva Antinori
(Toscana)

SARDE FRESCHE ALLA GRIGLIA

GRILLED FRESH SARDINES

If you have a wood or charcoal fire, use a fish holder to cook and turn the fish. Otherwise, use a cast iron grill pan.

12	fresh large sardines or fresh herrings	12		**FOR THE DRESSING**		
⅓ cup	extra virgin olive oil	75 mL		4 Tbsp	extra virgin olive oil	50 mL
⅓ cup	red wine vinegar	75 mL		2 Tbsp	balsamic or red wine vinegar	25 mL
6	cloves garlic, thinly sliced	6		1½ Tbsp	chopped fresh mint and fresh Italian parsley	20 mL
2 Tbsp	chopped fresh Italian parsley	25 mL				
1 Tbsp	chopped fresh mint	15 mL				
	Salt and pepper					

MENU SUGGESTION
For a main course, serve meats or pasta.

RECOMMENDED WINE
White. Pinot Grigio, La Cros, Valdadige, (Alto Adige); Masi Bianco, Serego Alighieri (Veneto)

∽ To clean, fillet, and butterfly the fish: Trim the fins off the sardines with a pair of scissors. Remove the scales by running the fish under water and loosening the scales with your hands. Cut along the belly with a sharp knife from the gut cavity to the tail and remove the guts. Cut off the head and open out the fish onto a flat surface, belly side down, and gently press along the backbone with your thumb to break the spine. Turn the fish over and remove the spine and any small bones that remain.

∽ Mix the olive oil, vinegar, garlic, parsley, mint, salt and pepper, add the fish and marinate for at least 1 hour. Drain before grilling.

∽ Make the dressing by combining the olive oil, vinegar and herbs.

∽ Grill the fish, skin side down until brown (the white begins to show on the top side); then grill the other side. Place the grilled fish on a dinner plate and top with the dressing.

∽ Add a few capers to taste and serve as an appetizer with a few grilled vegetables, such as Grilled Zucchini and Eggplant (page 61).

Serves 6

ZUCCHINE E MELENZANE GRIGLIATE

GRILLED ZUCCHINI AND EGGPLANT

The process of grilling the vegetables produces a delicious barbequed flavor with the vegetables cooked al dente and flavored with the vinaigrette.

1	medium eggplant	1	2 Tbsp	chopped fresh mint	25 mL
2	medium zucchini	2	2	cloves garlic, thinly sliced	2
	Salt		⅓ cup	extra virgin olive oil	75 mL
2 Tbsp	red wine vinegar (or to taste)	25 mL			

~ Wash the vegetables and slice them lengthwise ¼ inch (.6 cm) thick. Place a grill or cast iron grill pan over high heat. Sprinkle the surface of the pan with salt so that the vegetables do not stick. When the pan is hot, add half the eggplant and zucchini and sear for about 5 minutes. Turn over and sear the other side. Repeat the process with the remaining vegetables.

~ Combine the vinegar, mint, garlic and olive oil to make a vinaigrette dressing.

~ Place the vegetables in a serving dish and sprinkle lightly with salt. Drizzle the vinaigrette over the grilled vegetables.

NOTE: *Other vegetables can also be used, such as fennel and red peppers. The fennel and red peppers should be dressed with a basil vinaigrette (substitute basil for mint).*

Serves 4

RECOMMENDED WINE
*Red. Aglianico del Vulture,
D'Angelo (Basilicata)*

FUNGHI ALLA MILANESE

MUSHROOMS, MILANESE STYLE

These mushrooms make a delicious appetizer or side dish. I particularly like to use porcini mushrooms for this recipe.

8	medium mushroom caps: porcini, portobello or shiitake	8	¼ cup	extra virgin olive oil	50 mL
½ cup	flour	125 mL	¼ cup	unsalted butter	50 mL
2	eggs, well beaten	2		Juice of 1 lemon	
1 cup	fine breadcrumbs	250 mL		Salt	

RECOMMENDED WINE
White. Vintage Tunina, Jermann (Friuli-Venezia Giulia)

❧ Wash and dry the mushroom caps. Dredge the mushrooms in the flour, the egg, and the breadcrumbs consecutively. Heat the oil and butter in a pan and fry the mushrooms on both sides until golden (do not overcook). Immediately, place the mushrooms on a serving plate and sprinkle with fresh lemon juice and salt. Serve hot.

Serves 4

PEPERONI CON SALSA BAGNA CAUDA

PEPPERS WITH BAGNA CAUDA SAUCE

Bagna Cauda ("warm bath") a sauce from Piemonte in Italy, is usually served warm as a dip for vegetables. This sauce is often served with a variety of appetizers. This dish would go well with a second course of venison or pasta with a porcini mushroom sauce.

½ cup	extra virgin olive oil	125 mL	18	olives, pitted	18
3	cloves garlic, finely sliced	3	1 Tbsp	large capers (Lampedusa,	15 mL
4	mixed peppers stemmed, seeded	4		if possible)	
	and quartered		1 Tbsp	unsalted butter	15 mL
6	anchovy fillets	6			

Heat half the olive oil in a frying pan and add half the garlic and all of the peppers. Cook over medium-high heat. When the peppers are brown, remove them to a serving dish. In a clean pan, heat the remaining olive oil and saute the remaining garlic until it is light brown. Add the anchovies and olives; heat, then add the capers and stir until they are hot. Add the butter, stirring until melted. Arrange the peppers cut side up and pour the sauce over them. Serve with fresh bread.

Serves 4

RECOMMENDED WINE
White. Pinot Grigio, (Friuli-Venezia Giulia and Trentino-Alto Adige)

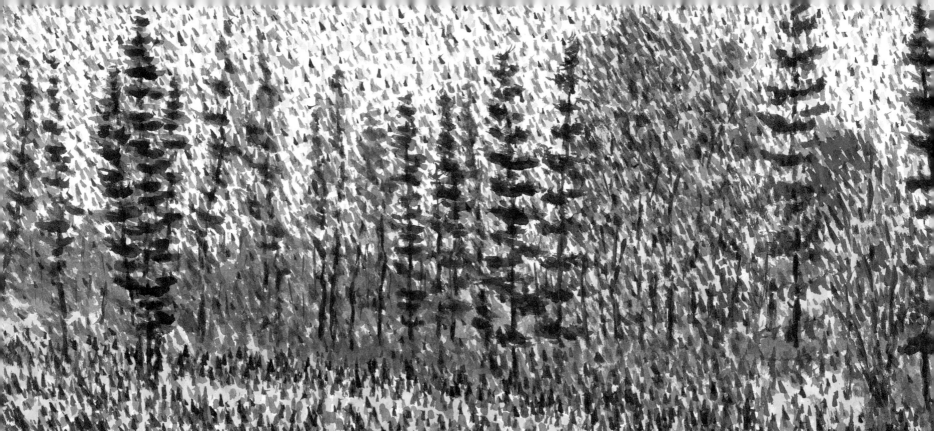

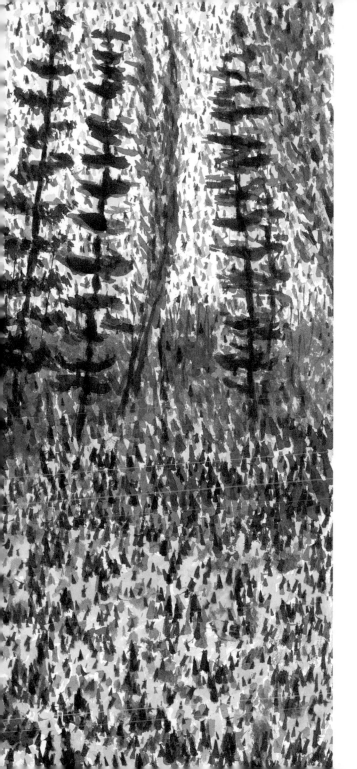

PASTAS AND RISOTTOS

RAGU ALLA CONTADINA

FARMER'S RAGU SAUCE

Serve with a mixed salad and Luigi's simple dressing, i.e., on top of the leaves, sprinkle some extra virgin olive oil, a little red wine vinegar and a few drops of water, salt and pepper, and toss.

7	cloves garlic, sliced	7	3	sprigs fresh basil	3
¼ cup	extra virgin olive oil	50 mL		Salt	
2 lbs	beef shanks	1 kg	4 Tbsp	unsalted butter	50 mL
2	13 oz (370 mL) cans tomato paste	2	1¾ lbs	fettuccine	800 g
8 cups	water	2 L		Parmigiano Reggiano cheese	
1	28 oz (796 mL) can peeled tomatoes, drained and crushed	1			

RECOMMENDED WINE
Red. Tignanello, Antinori (Toscana) Barbera d'Asti, Michele Chiarlo (Piemonte)

In a large 4-inch (10 cm) deep skillet, saute the garlic in the olive oil. When the garlic is light brown, add the beef shanks and saute until the meat is golden brown. Add the tomato paste and cook for 2 minutes, stirring to remove the acidity. Add the water, tomatoes, basil and salt to taste; simmer slowly until the meat falls from the bones and is tender, approximately 2 hours. Add more water if the sauce becomes too thick.

Remove the meat with a slotted spoon and set aside. Return the sauce to the stove and add the butter. When the butter has melted, the sauce is ready; remove it from the stove and set aside.

Bring a pot of salted water to a boil. Add the pasta and cook until al dente.

To serve, drain the pasta; pool some sauce on a plate and top it with cheese, then fettuccine, and finish with sauce and additional Parmesan. This sauce is also used for the Ravioli with Sweetbreads, Lombardy Style (page 78).

Serve the meat on the side topped with a little sauce, or serve it another day for lunch with a salad.

Serves 8

FETTUCCINE ALLA PANNA

FETTUCCINE WITH CREAM

We were on our way to San Remo, the last port of call on the west side of the Italian Riviera, when the wind picked up and rain threatened. The captain reviewed the chart and saw that we could go directly into a large new marina at Degli Aregai, just north of the village of San Stephano, and not a moment too soon. The wind was blowing thirty-five knots when we entered the harbor. The small village of San Stephano was only two kilometers away, so I went scouting for provisions for dinner. I was pleasantly surprised to find outstanding food supplies in this small, quaint village, including dried porcini linguine noodles, "specialita gastronomica", from "Piemonteiss". It was with this special noodle that I served fettuccine with cream sauce along with a panfried veal chop sauteed in Marsala wine, and, of course, a bottle of Tignanello.

⅓ cup	unsalted butter	75 mL	1 Tbsp	finely chopped fresh Italian parsley	15 mL
1½ cups	whipping cream (35%)	375 mL			
1 lb	fresh egg fettuccine, or dried porcini linguine noodles	500 g	⅓ cup	grated Parmigiano Reggiano cheese	75 mL
1	egg yolk, optional	1			

↝ Heat the butter and cream in a large skillet until they almost reach a boil. Keep warm and reheat just prior to adding the cooked fettuccine.

↝ In a separate pot, bring 8 cups (2 L) of salted water to a boil; add the pasta and stir constantly for 3 minutes if it is fresh pasta, or 8 minutes if it is dried, until al dente. Remove the pot from the heat, drop 1 cup (250 mL) of cold water into the pasta water and stir to stop the cooking. Drain.

↝ Reheat the sauce. Add the egg yolk, if using, and stir until the sauce has reached desired thickness. Stir the cooked fettuccine into the sauce.

↝ Remove the skillet from the heat and add the parsley and cheese. Serve with additional cheese on the side.

Serves 4

RECOMMENDED WINE
Red. Cabernet Sauvignon Ferrata, Maculan (Veneto) Cabernet Sauvignon, Principe di Corleone (Sicilia) Tignanello, Antinori (Toscana)

LINGUINE PORTO DI MOLA

LINGUINE FROM FORMIA

We were sailing the southern Italian Lazio coast, and the weather forecast predicted strong winds, so we wanted a secure place to moor the boat that night. The pilot indicated two ports nearby, Gaeta and Formia. We chose Formia, a large modern town with very few tourists, and we liked it very much. As well, the boat was moored directly in front of a well known restaurant, the Zi Anna Mare, and the fish market was a few steps away. Everything we wanted! The next night a boat with a British flag entered the harbor in strong winds. We helped the couple moor their boat and invited them over for a drink. Drinks led to dinner. I had purchased fillets of fresh sardines that morning and I wanted to try out this recipe. I served a white Pinot Grigio wine and awaited the response . . . it was a hit. The blend of tastes of the sardines and the mint is exciting, and the wine goes perfectly.

4	cloves garlic, chopped	4		Salt	
4 Tbsp	extra virgin olive oil	50 mL	1 Tbsp	capers	15 mL
1 lb	fresh sardines or herrings	500 g	1½ tsp	green peppercorns	8 mL
	(see page 60 to prepare sardines)		1 lb	linguine	500 g
½ cup	dry white wine	125 mL	3	sprigs fresh mint, chopped	3
1¼ lbs	fresh or canned tomatoes, peeled and seeded	600 g			

MENU SUGGESTION
As a main course, serve with Black Sea Bass in Black Butter.

RECOMMENDED WINE
*White. Cervaro della Sala, Antinori (Umbria)
Greco di Tufo, Mastroberardino (Campania)*

↝ In a large skillet, saute the garlic in the olive oil until just brown; add the sardines and slowly add the white wine, a little at a time. Add the tomatoes and cook for 10 minutes; add salt, capers and peppercorns.

↝ In a separate pot, bring salted water to a boil; add the linguine and cook halfway. Drain the pasta, and finish cooking it in the sauce. Serve immediately topped with chopped mint.

Serves 6

LINGUINE AL BRODETTO D'ASTICE

LINGUINE IN LIGHT LOBSTER SAUCE

1¼ lbs	live lobster	600 g	2 Tbsp	chopped fresh Italian parsley	25 mL
⅓ cup	extra virgin olive oil	75 mL	1	whole green onion, finely chopped	1
3	cloves garlic, sliced	3	¼ tsp	dried chili peppers, or more	1 mL
½ cup	dry white wine	125 mL		to taste	
6	fresh tomatoes or canned	6		Salt and pepper	
	tomatoes, peeled and seeded		½ lb	dried linguine or spaghettini	250 g
6	fresh basil leaves, chopped	6	1 Tbsp	unsalted butter	15 mL

〜 Cut the lobster in half lengthwise with a meat cleaver and remove the sac near the head all the way down to the tail. Crack the claws (or have the fishmonger do this for you). Saute the lobster, shell and all, in three-quarters of the olive oil and all of the garlic; add the wine and reduce. Add the tomatoes, basil, parsley, green onion, chili peppers, salt and pepper. Cook for 20 minutes over medium heat; remove the shells. (This dish can be made ahead of time to this point and rewarmed just before adding pasta.)

〜 Cook the pasta until al dente. Drain. Add the cooked pasta and butter to the lobster sauce and cook for about 40 seconds. Serve topped with the remaining olive oil and fresh parsley.

Serves 2

RECOMMENDED WINE
White. Inama Soave Classico Superiore, Vigneti di Foscarino (Veneto)

FUNGHI CON POMODORI

MUSHROOM SAUCE WITH TOMATOES

This rich, earthy, mushroom sauce goes well with Medallions of Veal with Sage.

1 lb	fresh porcini or portobello mushrooms	500 g	1⅔ cups	fresh tomatoes or canned tomatoes	400 mL
½ cup	extra virgin olive oil	125 mL	1 Tbsp	flour	15 mL
1	onion, finely chopped	1	¼ cup	unsalted butter	50 mL
4	cloves garlic, finely chopped	4		Salt and pepper	
1	carrot, finely chopped	1	1 lb	dried egg tagliatelle	500 g
1	rib celery, finely chopped	1		Parmigiano Reggiano cheese	
3 Tbsp	fresh Italian parsley leaves	45 mL			

∽ Wipe the mushroom caps with a damp paper towel and discard the stems; thinly slice the mushroom caps. In a large skillet, heat half the olive oil and saute the onion, garlic, carrot and celery until the vegetables are transparent. Add the parsley leaves and stir; then add the mushrooms and cook for 10 minutes. Add the tomatoes and cook for 10 minutes more. Mix the flour with the butter and stir into the sauce. Season with salt and pepper to taste, then cook for 5 minutes.

∽ Meanwhile, cook the pasta in a large pot of boiling salted water until al dente. Drain. Pour the sauce and the remaining olive oil over the pasta. Serve with cheese.

Serves 4

FUNGHI SALTATI

SAUTEED MUSHROOMS FOR PASTA

Follow the method above but omit tomatoes. Instead, add ⅓ cup (75 mL) white wine after sauteing the vegetables and cook until the wine has evaporated. Proceed as above.

RECOMMENDED WINE
Red. Teroldego Rotaliano, Mezzacorona (Trentino-Alto Adige)

SALSA DI POMODORO ALLA NAPOLETANA

NEAPOLITAN TOMATO SAUCE

Green pepper, black beans and corn can be added to create a delicious salsa that can be served with blue corn chips or scrambled eggs.

⅓ cup	extra virgin olive oil	75 mL	12	fresh basil leaves	12
1	onion, chopped	1		Salt and pepper	
3	large cloves garlic, crushed	3	1¼ lbs	dried spaghetti or fettuccine	600 g
2¼ lbs	tomatoes, chopped	1 kg			
2 Tbsp	pine nuts	25 mL			

MENU SUGGESTION
For a main course, serve grilled fish or Fish Soup from the Gulf of Gaeta .

RECOMMENDED WINE
Red. Falerno, (Campania) Rubesco (Umbria)

In a large skillet, heat the olive oil and saute the onion and the garlic until the onion is transparent. Add the tomatoes, pine nuts, basil, salt and pepper. Cook slowly, uncovered, for approximately 15 minutes, or until the water has evaporated and the oil floats free from the tomato.

Meanwhile, cook the pasta in a large pot of boiling salted water until al dente. Drain, toss with the sauce and serve.

Serves 6

PESTO ALLA GENOVESE

PASTA WITH FRESH BASIL SAUCE (PESTO)

Pasta with pesto sauce is very rich and is typically served as a first course.

1	bunch fresh basil, about 15 leaves (no stems)	1	¼ cup	grated Parmigiano Reggiano cheese	50 mL
1	handful of fresh baby spinach leaves	1	⅓ cup	grated Pecorino cheese	75 mL
			5 Tbsp	extra virgin olive oil	75 mL
2 Tbsp	fresh Italian parsley	25 mL		Salt	
3	cloves garlic, chopped	3	1½ oz	pine nuts	40 g

Basil and spinach should be clean and dry. Place basil leaves, spinach and parsley in a food processor and blend to a paste. Add the remaining ingredients and continue blending until the sauce is smooth. Serve with spaghettini or linguine.

Serves 2

RECOMMENDED WINE
White. Cinqueterre (Liguria)
Red. Rosso Piceno (Marche)

La Fenice

PASTA CON SALSA DI NOCI

PASTA WITH WALNUT SAUCE

Pasta with walnut sauce is rich and is best served as a first course. For a main course, serve duck, poultry or game.

½ cup	walnut pieces	125 mL			Salt	
¼ cup	pine nuts	50 mL	¾ lb		gnocchi, fettuccine or lasagne	400 g
3 Tbsp	extra virgin olive oil	45 mL				
2 Tbsp	chopped fresh Italian parsley	25 mL				

RECOMMENDED WINE
*Rosé. Rosato di Bolgheri
(Toscana)
White. Cervaro della Sala,
Antinori (Umbria)*

~ In a food processor, finely chop the nuts. Heat the olive oil and saute the nuts and parsley, stirring constantly, for 3 minutes. Add salt to taste and additional oil, if desired.

~ Cook the pasta in boiling salted water until al dente. Add the pasta to the walnut sauce and toss until mixed. Serve.

Serves 4

PENNE ALLA PUTTANESCA

PENNE WITH PUTTANESCA SAUCE

½ cup	extra virgin olive oil	125 mL	¾ cup	Kalamata olives, pitted and halved	175 mL
1	small onion, chopped	1			
4	cloves garlic, chopped	4	2 Tbsp	capers	25 mL
¼ tsp	dried chili peppers	1 mL	1 lb	dried penne	500 g
6	anchovy fillets	6		grated Parmigiano Reggiano cheese, optional	
28 oz	can tomatoes	796 mL			

In a large skillet, heat the olive oil. Saute the onions until transparent; add the garlic and saute until light brown. Add the chili peppers and stir. Add the anchovies and remove the pan from the heat. Stir the mixture until the anchovies are completely melted.

Return the pan to the heat and add the tomatoes and their juice. Bring to a slow boil then lower the heat and simmer for about 20 minutes, or until the tomatoes separate from the oil. Add the olives and heat until warm, then add the capers and stir.

Cook the penne in boiling salted water until al dente. Drain well. Mix the penne into the sauce and heat through. Serve with Parmesan cheese on the side, if desired.

Serves 4

RECOMMENDED WINE
Red. Amarone (Veneto)
Rosso del Conte (Sicilia)

RAVIOLI FARCITI CON CARNE D'ARAGOSTA

RAVIOLI WITH LOBSTER

This is a fabulous recipe and, if you have never tackled homemade pasta before, it's an enjoyable way to spend an afternoon and impress your guests for dinner.

FOR THE RAVIOLI DOUGH

4	eggs	4
3 cups	flour	750 mL
2	egg whites, beaten	2

FOR THE FILLING

2	cloves garlic, crushed	2
¼ cup	extra virgin olive oil	50 mL
1¼ lbs	fresh raw lobster meat, with egg sacs and shells	600 g
2 Tbsp	chopped fresh Italian parsley	25 mL
⅓ cup	dry white wine	75 mL
⅓ cup	fresh fine breadcrumbs	75 mL
1 tsp	chopped fresh dill	5 mL
	Salt and pepper	

FOR THE LOBSTER SAUCE

	reserved lobster shells	
3 Tbsp	extra virgin olive oil	45 mL
2	cloves garlic, chopped	2
⅓ cup	dry white wine	75 mL
4	fresh tomatoes, peeled, seeded and chopped	4
1 Tbsp	chopped fresh Italian parsley	15 mL
¼ tsp	dried chili peppers	1 mL
	Salt and pepper	

RECOMMENDED WINE
*White. Greco di Tufo,
Mastroberardino (Campania)*

Mound the flour on a work surface. Make a hole in the center of the flour and break the eggs into the hole. Beat the eggs lightly with a fork. Mix the eggs into the flour a little at a time. Work the flour and eggs together until the mixture is fully integrated and no longer moist. Gather the dough into a ball and let it rest for 1 hour. Dust the work surface with flour and roll the dough very thinly or put it through a pasta machine. Alternately, buy fresh sheets of egg pasta at a pasta shop, but be sure the sheets are thin.

In a large skillet, saute the garlic in the olive oil until light brown. Add the lobster meat, half the parsley and all of the wine; reduce completely over moderate heat. Finely chop the lobster meat and mix it with any liquid left in the skillet, the breadcrumbs, remaining parsley, dill, egg whites, salt and pepper.

~ Brush the sheets of pasta with the egg whites. Place spoonfuls of the filling on a sheet of pasta about 1½ inches (3.75 cm) apart. Brush a second sheet of pasta with the egg whites and cover the first sheet. Use a knife to cut out the ravioli. Make sure the edges of each ravioli are pressed together.

~ Cook the ravioli in boiling salted water for about 3 minutes. Drain.

~ Saute the lobster shells in the olive oil, garlic and wine until the liquid is reduced by half. Add the tomatoes, parsley, chili peppers, salt and pepper. Simmer for 20 minutes. Remove the lobster shells.

~ Add the cooked ravioli to the sauce and cook on high heat for 10 to 15 seconds. Serve immediately.

Serves 4

RAVIOLI D'ANIMELLE ALLA LOMBARDA

RAVIOLI WITH SWEETBREADS, LOMBARDY STYLE

This recipe works beautifully with the Farmer's Ragu Sauce (page 66) or the following herb sauce.

1	Ravioli Dough recipe (page 76)	1		2	egg yolks, slightly beaten	2
	FOR THE FILLING				Nutmeg	
2 cups	veal sweetbreads	500 g			Salt and pepper	
2 Tbsp	extra virgin olive oil	25 mL				
2 Tbsp	unsalted butter	25 mL			FOR THE HERB SAUCE	
¾ cup	coarse breadcrumbs, soaked in milk and strained	175 mL		⅓ cup	unsalted butter	75 mL
¾ cup	beef marrow (see Note)	175 g		8	fresh sage leaves	8
1⅔ cups	cooked, diced chicken meat	400 g		1	sprig fresh rosemary, leaves removed from stem	1
½ cup	grated Parmigiano Reggiano cheese	125 mL			Parmigiano Reggiano cheese	

MENU SUGGESTION
Serve with steamed vegetables with extra virgin olive oil and lemon; or green beans all'agro (oil and lemon).

RECOMMENDED WINE
Red (with the Ragu Sauce).
Cannonau di Sardegna, Riserva (Sardegna)
Frizzante (with the Herb Sauce).
Freisa, secco, Giacomo Bologna (Piemonte)
Tenutas Anna, Cabernet, Vino Spumante (Veneto)

～ Make the ravioli dough.

～ Boil the sweetbreads in water for about 30 minutes. Cool, and remove the skins. Finely dice the sweetbreads and saute them in the olive oil and butter. Add the breadcrumbs and beef marrow and cook for 15 minutes on high heat. Blend in a food processor with the cooked chicken and Parmesan cheese for 30 seconds. Add the egg yolks, nutmeg, salt and pepper, and more breadcrumbs if necessary, and mix.

～ Fill the ravioli as on page 77. Cook the ravioli in boiling salted water for about 3 minutes.

～ Reserve 1 cup (250 mL) of the cooking water, if using herb sauce.

～ To make the sauce, melt the butter, add the reserved cooking water before the butter is completely melted. Add the herbs and stir. Drain the ravioli, add to the herb sauce, and saute for 2 minutes. Add Parmesan cheese to taste.

～ Place the ravioli on a serving dish and top with sauce.

NOTE: *Ask your butcher to give you beef shank bones with large marrows. Place the bones in a pot of boiling water and cook until the marrow is soft. Remove the marrow from the bones and reserve. Discard the bones.*

Serves 8

RISOTTO CON ASPARAGI

RISOTTO WITH ASPARAGUS

¼ cup	extra virgin olive oil	50 mL	2 Tbsp	unsalted butter	25 mL
1	small onion, finely chopped	1		Salt and pepper	
16	asparagus spears trimmed	16	¼ cup	grated Parmigiano Reggiano	50 mL
1 cup	Italian short grain rice, unwashed	250 mL		cheese	
2¼ cups	½ homemade chicken stock and ½ water (as needed)	500 mL			

In a large saucepan, heat the olive oil over moderate heat. Add the onion and saute until it is transparent. Add 8 spears of asparagus, cut into 1-inch (2.5 cm) pieces and cook for 1 minute. Add the rice and mix. Add 1 cup (250 mL) of the stock to the rice mixture and cook, stirring slowly and continuously until the liquid is absorbed. Continue to add the rest of the stock, a little at a time, until the rice is al dente and creamy. Add the butter and stir for 1 minute. Add salt and pepper. Remove from the heat.

Toss the remaining 8 spears of asparagus with a little olive oil and grill them.

To serve, place the risotto on a serving plate and top with the grilled asparagus spears and Parmesan cheese. Place under a grill for a few minutes and serve immediately.

Serves 4

RECOMMENDED WINE
Red. Ferrata, Maculan (Veneto) Cabernet Sauvignon
White. Ferrata, Maculan (Veneto) Chardonnay

RISOTTO CON RADICCHIO

RISOTTO WITH RADICCHIO

Serve as an appetizer or as a side dish.

16	leaves of Trevisano radicchio	16	¼ cup	unsalted butter	50 mL
¼ cup	extra virgin olive oil	50 mL		Salt and pepper	
1	small onion, finely chopped	1	¼ cup	grated Parmigiano Reggiano	50 mL
1 cup	Italian short grain rice, unwashed	250 mL		cheese	
2¼ cups	½ homemade chicken stock and ½ water (as needed)	500 mL			

RECOMMENDED WINE
*Red. Barbera d'Alba, Luigi
Einaudi (Piemonte)
Cabernet Terre di Franciacorta
(Lombardia)*

∾ Reserve the best 4 radicchio leaves for grilling and garnish. Toss with a little olive oil, grill in a hot cast iron grill pan and set aside.

∾ Cut 8 of the remaining radicchio leaves into large julienne.

∾ In a large saucepan, heat the olive oil over moderate heat. Add the onion and saute until it is transparent. Add the julienned radicchio and cook for 1 minute. Add the rice and mix. Add 1 cup (250 mL) of the stock to the rice mixture and cook, stirring slowly and continuously, until the liquid is absorbed. Continue to add the rest of the stock, a little at a time, until the rice is al dente and creamy. Add the butter, salt and pepper and stir for 1 minute. Remove from the heat.

∾ To serve, use one raw, whole radicchio leaf per serving. Form each leaf into a heart shape on a plate and top with the risotto, cheese and a grilled radicchio leaf.

Serves 4

RISOTTO CON SCAMPI

RISOTTO WITH SCAMPI

Serve with a salad if serving the risotto as a main course, but this recipe also makes a good first course.

1	medium onion, finely chopped	1	1 cup	dry white wine	250 mL
1	carrot, finely chopped	1	4½ cups	fish stock, preferably homemade	1 L
1	rib celery, finely chopped	1	1¼ lbs	scampi	600 g
⅓ cup	extra virgin olive oil	75 mL	3 cups	Italian short grain rice, preferably	750 g
¾ cup	unsalted butter	175 mL		Riso Vialone Nano, washed once	
3 Tbsp	brandy	45 mL		Chopped fresh Italian parsley	

➤ In a 3-quart (3 L) pot, saute the onion, carrot and celery in the olive oil and butter until the onion is transparent. Add the brandy and white wine and reduce until most of the liquid has evaporated.

➤ Bring the fish stock to a gentle simmer (keep it simmering all through the cooking of the rice).

➤ Shell and clean the scampi and chop coarsely. Add the scampi to the vegetables and simmer for about 6 minutes.

➤ Wash the rice once (some starch is required). Add the rice to the scampi and vegetables. Add the fish stock, ½ cup (125 mL) at a time, and stir constantly over medium heat until the liquid is absorbed by the rice. Continue adding stock until the rice is creamy and al dente. Place the risotto on a serving dish and sprinkle with parsley.

Serves 8

RECOMMENDED WINE
White. Mastroberardino, either Greco di Tufo or Fiano d'Avellino (Campania)

RISOTTO ALLA PESCATORE

RISOTTO WITH SEAFOOD

If serving the Risotto with Seafood as a first course, follow with a main course of red snapper.

1½ cups	fish stock, preferably homemade	375 mL	½ cup	fresh or canned tomatoes, finely chopped	125 mL
2	cloves garlic, chopped	2		Salt	
¼ cup	extra virgin olive oil	50 mL		Pepper (jalapeno, if desired)	
12	small shrimp, unpeeled	12	1½ cups	Italian short grain rice, preferably Riso Vialone Nano, washed once	375 mL
12	medium clams, preferably Manila	12			
12	mussels	12			
4	small squid, cleaned and cut into rings	4	2 Tbsp	chopped fresh Italian parsley	25 mL
4	small cuttlefish, coarsely chopped	4			
⅓ cup	white wine	75 mL			

RECOMMENDED WINE

White. Sauvignon Ronco di Mele, Venica & Venica (Friuli-Venezia Giulia)

∾ Bring the fish stock to a gentle simmer (keep it simmering while cooking the rice).

∾ In a large skillet, over high heat, saute the garlic in the olive oil until the garlic is light brown. Add the fish and saute for 1½ minutes. Add the jalapeno, if using. Add the wine, tomatoes, salt and pepper and reduce the liquid by half. Add the rice and stir until well mixed with the seafood. Add the fish stock and cook, stirring continuously, until the liquid is absorbed. Cover with a lid for a short time, if necessary, to open the clams. Add a little water, if necessary, until the rice is cooked al dente.

∾ To serve, remove the clams and mussels first, placing them on the outside of the plate, then place the remaining rice and seafood in the center of the plate. Sprinkle with parsley and serve.

Serves 4

GAMBERI ALLA FRA DIAVOLO

SHRIMP ALLA FRA DIAVOLO

16	medium shrimps	16	2	sprigs fresh Italian parsley	2
4	cloves fresh garlic, crushed	4	1⅔ cup	fish stock, preferably	400 mL
¾ cup	extra virgin olive oil	175 mL		homemade	
¾ cup	dry white wine	175 mL		Salt	
4	fresh tomatoes, peeled, seeded	4	1 lb	spaghettini or spaghetti	500 g
	and chopped		2 Tbsp	chopped parsley	25 mL

⌁ To prepare the shrimp, cut the shells down the back to the tails and devein. The shells can be added to the cooking liquid for more flavor, but they must be removed before the pasta is added. Wash the shrimp in cold water and dry on paper towels.

⌁ In a large skillet, brown the garlic in ½ cup (125 mL) of the olive oil. Add the shrimp and saute lightly (1 or 2 minutes). Add the wine and reduce by half. To avoid overcooking the shrimp, remove when cooked and continue to reduce the wine. Add the tomatoes and cook for about 3 minutes; add the parsley, fish stock and salt and boil moderately for another 5 minutes. Remove the garlic before adding the pasta.

⌁ In a separate pot, bring salted water to a boil; add the pasta and cook it halfway. Drain the pasta, reserving some of the cooking water.

⌁ Place the partially cooked pasta in the skillet with the sauce and finish cooking the pasta until it is al dente, adding the reserved pasta water, if necessary, to avoid burning.

⌁ Return the shrimp to the pasta sauce just before serving and warm for 30 seconds. Place the pasta in a serving dish or individual bowls and drizzle with the remaining ¼ cup (50 mL) of olive oil and chopped parsley.

Serves 4

RECOMMENDED WINE
Red. Chianti Classico, Riserva (Toscana)
White. Sauvignon Ronco di Mele, Venica & Venica (Friuli-Venezia Giulia)

SPAGHETTI AGLIO E OLIO E PEPERONCINO

SPAGHETTI WITH GARLIC, OIL AND HOT PEPPER

This is the traditional pasta dish that Ricardo Muti enjoyed at La Fenice and recommended to his friends in the orchestra.

14 oz	spaghetti	400 g	Black pepper
4	cloves garlic, crushed	4	Chopped fresh Italian parsley
3	anchovy fillets	3	Dried chili peppers
½ cup	extra virgin olive oil	125 mL	

RECOMMENDED WINE
Red. Cannonau di Sardegna, Riserva (Sardegna)

∾ Cook the pasta in boiling, salted water for 6 minutes. Drain the pasta, reserving ⅓ cup (75 mL) of the cooking water.

∾ Brown the garlic and the anchovies in the olive oil for 2 minutes, stirring the anchovies until they are almost completely melted. Add the chili peppers, stir, then add the pasta all at once and the water, a little at a time. Saute, stirring constantly until all the water is absorbed by the pasta. Make sure the pasta is cooked al dente.

∾ Sprinkle with freshly ground pepper, and parsley and chili peppers.

Serves 4

SPAGHETTINI AL FILETTO DI POMODORI CON BASILICO

SPAGHETTINI WITH BASIL AND TOMATO

This pasta is a fabulous specialty of La Fenice.

½ cup	extra virgin olive oil	125 mL	10	fresh basil leaves	10
3	cloves garlic, crushed	3		Salt	
6	medium tomatoes, or 28 oz (796 mL) canned tomatoes, drained	6	¾ lb	spaghettini	400 g

~ Heat half the olive oil in a large skillet and saute the garlic until it is light brown. Add the tomatoes, thinly sliced, or squeezed by hand if canned, half the basil leaves and salt. Cook over moderate heat for 4 minutes if using fresh tomatoes, or for 10 minutes if using canned tomatoes. Remove from the heat. Remove the garlic, if you wish.

~ Cook the spaghettini in boiling salted water until it is nearly al dente. Drain.

~ Return the sauce to the heat and, when it is simmering, add the spaghettini and cook for 1 minute. Place in a serving dish, pour the remaining olive oil over the spaghettini and sprinkle with the remaining basil leaves. You can also add some arugula, as an alternative, or an addition, to the basil. Serve.

Serves 4

RECOMMENDED WINE

Red. Chianti Classico, Badia a Passignano, Reserva, Antinori (Toscana)

SPAGHETTINI CON VONGOLE

SPAGHETTINI WITH CLAM SAUCE

I have loved Pasta Con Vongole for years. When I visited Italy and ate the special clam sauce of Formia, where the noodles embraced the taste of the clams, I was desperate to learn the method from Luigi. Luigi gave me the simple secret: add the partially cooked noodles to the broth and then finish the cooking together! (The Manilla clams are closer to the vongole veraci served in Italy.)

48	Manilla clams	48	1 lb	spaghettini or linguine	500 g
⅓ cup	extra virgin olive oil	75 mL	3 Tbsp	chopped fresh Italian parsley	45 mL
3	cloves garlic, finely chopped	3			
¼ tsp	dried chili peppers, or 1 fresh jalapeno pepper	1 mL			

RECOMMENDED WINE

White. Verdicchio, Marchetti (Marche)
Gavi "La Raja" Martinengo (Piemonte)

꙼ Scrub the clams to remove dirt, and rinse in several changes of cold water.

꙼ Place them in a bowl topped with ice cubes, and refrigerate. Drain when ready to use.

꙼ In a 4-inch (10 cm) deep skillet, heat half the olive oil and saute the garlic until light brown. Add the chili peppers with half the parsley and stir. Add the clams and ⅓ cup (75 mL) water and cook, covered, over high heat until the clams open. Remove the skillet from the heat.

꙼ In a separate pot, bring salted water to a boil, and half-cook the pasta. Drain.

꙼ Remove the clams from the pot and place them around a large serving dish, leaving space in the center for the pasta. Put the partially cooked pasta in the skillet with the clam sauce. Saute over high heat until the liquid is almost absorbed and slightly thickened, and the pasta is cooked al dente. Place the pasta in the serving dish with the clams. Drizzle with the remaining olive oil and sprinkle with parsley.

꙼ For Red Clam Sauce: Follow the above directions, adding the pulp of 2 tomatoes when adding the clams.

Serves 4

TAGLIATELLE ALL'ERBETTE

TAGLIATELLE WITH HERBS

The tagliatelle noodle is a little broader than fettuccine. Ruchetta is similar to arugula, but is a wild herb with a richer, nuttier flavor. It may be found at quality food stores or Italian markets. For a second course, serve fowl, lamb or veal.

8	fresh sage leaves, coarsely chopped	8	8	leaves ruchetta, or arugula, coarsely chopped	8
2	sprigs fresh rosemary	2			
1	sprig fresh Italian parsley, coarsely chopped	1	⅓ cup	unsalted butter	75 mL
			1 lb	egg tagliatelle	500 g
4	leaves fresh basil, coarsely chopped	4	½ cup	grated Parmigiano Reggiano cheese	125 mL
1	sprig fresh thyme	1			

✎ Wash and clean the herbs and remove the stems. Wash the ruchetta, or arugula, and cut the stems off where the leaves begin.

✎ In a separate pan, half-cook the pasta in boiling salted water. Drain, reserving some of the cooking water.

✎ To a large skillet, add ½ ladle of the pasta water, the herbs and the ruchetta, or arugula. Add the butter and bring to a boil; adjust for salt. Put the tagliatelle in the saucepan with the herbs; mix together and cook until the pasta is al dente. If the sauce becomes dry, add some of the reserved pasta water. Remove from the heat. Add the cheese, toss and serve immediately.

Serves 4

RECOMMENDED WINE
*Light Red. Valpolicella Classico, Boscaini (Veneto)
White. Prosecco di Valdobbiadene, a white frizzante (Veneto)*

FISH AND SEAFOOD

FUMETTO DI PESCE

FISH STOCK

This fish stock can be used for Shrimp alla Fra diavolo, Risotto with Scampi, Risotto with Seafood and Fish Soup from the Gulf of Gaeta.

⅓ cup	extra virgin olive oil	75 mL	2	ribs celery, crushed	2
2	medium onions, thinly sliced	2	6	sprigs fresh Italian parsley	6
6	cloves garlic, thinly sliced	6	1 Tbsp	green peppercorns	15 mL
4	fresh, medium-size fish heads (white)	4	2	fresh tomatoes, not ripe, sliced in 8 pieces	2
¾ cup	white wine	175 mL	4	bay leaves	4
8 cups	water, or enough to cover the ingredients	2 L		Salt to taste	

∾ In a stockpot, or other deep pot, warm the olive oil over medium heat and saute the onions and garlic until slightly brown. Add the fish heads and saute for about 8 minutes, being careful not to burn the fish. Pour in the wine and simmer until it is reduced by half. Add the water and the remaining ingredients, except the salt. Bring to a boil and continue to cook at a simmer for 1½ hours, until the liquid is slightly reduced and has the appearance of a fish broth. Add the salt.

∾ Strain the stock through cheesecloth into another pot. Let the stock cool and then place it in the refrigerator overnight. The next day, remove the excess fat. The stock is now ready to use or freeze.

Yield 6 cups (1.5 L)

PESCE AL FORNO CON SALSA DI FINOCCHIO

BAKED FISH WITH FENNEL SAUCE

FOR THE FENNEL SAUCE

2	whole fennel bulbs with green leaves	2
¼ cup	unsalted butter	50 mL
1	whole shallot, chopped	1
1 cup	fish stock, preferably homemade	250 mL
1 tsp	corn starch	5 mL
¼ cup	dry white wine	50 mL
10	threads saffron	10
	Juice of ½ a lemon	

4	medium fillets of white fish (sea bass, stripped bass, red snapper)	4
2	medium zucchini, sliced thinly lengthwise	2
1 Tbsp	finely chopped fresh rosemary, or coriander	15 mL
1 Tbsp	finely chopped fresh Italian parsley	15 mL
2 Tbsp	unsalted butter	25 mL
	Salt and pepper	

～ Preheat an oven to 350°F (180°C).

～ Remove the green leaves from both fennel bulbs. Finely chop the the green leaves and reserve. Coarsely chop one fennel bulb and puree in a food processor. Slice the other fennel bulb.

～ Put half the butter in a skillet; add the sliced fennel and the shallot and cook for 3 minutes; slowly add the fish stock and cook for 15 minutes. Before the liquid is completely evaporated, add the pureed fennel pulp, corn starch, wine and saffron and cook for an additional 4 minutes. Add the remaining butter and cook for 1 minute. Add the reserved finely chopped green leaves and mix. Add the lemon juice and simmer for 2 minutes more. Serve the sauce at room temperature.

～ Place the uncooked fish in a baking dish and sprinkle the fish with salt and pepper. Lay the slices of zucchini on top lengthwise and sprinkle with a mixture of the herbs. Dot with butter and bake until the fish is cooked. Serve with the fennel sauce.

Serves 4

RECOMMENDED WINE
White. Masi Bianco, Serego Alighieri (Veneto)

PESCE PERSICO AL BURRO NERO

BLACK SEA BASS IN BLACK BUTTER

Black sea bass can be found at Chinese markets. Serve with boiled potatoes, green beans and slivered carrots.

¼ cup	extra virgin olive oil	50 mL		FOR THE SAUCE:		
6	whole black sea bass or perch, 7 oz (200 g) each	6	½ cup	unsalted butter	125 mL	
4	green onions, crushed	4	2 Tbsp	fresh thyme	25 mL	
1	rib celery	1	2 Tbsp	chopped fresh Italian parsley	25 mL	
3	bay leaves	3	1 Tbsp	unsalted capers in brine, rinsed and chopped	15 mL	
2	sprigs fresh Italian parsley	2	2	lemons, cut in 6 wedges each		2
1 Tbsp	green peppercorns	15 mL		Salt		
	Salt to taste					

RECOMMENDED WINE

White. Gavi Fornaci del Tassarolo, Chiarlo (Piemonte) Chardonnay, Lungarotti (Umbria)

∽ Coat the bottom of a deep pan or heatproof casserole with half the olive oil and arrange the fish on top. Place the green onions, celery, bay leaves, parsley, remaining olive oil and green peppercorns on the fish. Add water to barely cover and sprinkle with salt. Simmer slowly on top of the stove, covered, for 10 minutes, or until the fish is just cooked. Remove the fish and place in a serving dish.

∽ To make the sauce, in a separate pan brown the butter over high heat then stir in the herbs and capers. Pour the hot sauce over the fish and serve immediately with lemon wedges on the side.

Serves 3

MERLUZZO CON SALSA PICCANTE

COD WITH SPICY SAUCE

Start with Crespelle or Pasta with Pesto. With any of these appetizers, you can serve the same wine.

FOR THE FIRST SAUCE

¼ cup	extra virgin olive oil	50 mL
2 Tbsp	red wine vinegar	25 mL
2 tsp	Dijon mustard	10 mL
2 tsp	small capers	10mL
2	small gherkin pickles, finely chopped	2
½	jalapeno pepper, finely chopped	½
1	small red onion, finely chopped	1
	Salt and pepper	

FOR THE SECOND SAUCE

2	hard-boiled eggs, finely chopped	2
1 tsp	chopped mint	5 mL
1 tsp	chopped dill	5 mL

1 Tbsp	chopped Italian parsley	15 mL
1 Tbsp	chives, chopped	15 mL
	Seasonal vegetables, such as:	
½ lb	green beans	250 g
8	young leeks	8
½ lb	young mini carrots	250 g
3 Tbsp	unsalted butter	45 mL
	Salt and pepper	
4	pieces fresh fillet of cod 5 oz (150 g) each, cleaned, scaled and deboned	4
2 cups	fish stock, preferably home- made, with juice of ½ a lemon added to the stock	500 mL

- Mix the ingredients for the first sauce in a bowl and set aside.

- Mix the eggs and herbs for the second sauce in a bowl and set aside.

- In a large pan, blanch the vegetables in boiling salted water until al dente; place under cold running water to stop the cooking. Lightly saute the vegetables in butter.

- In a large skillet, poach the cod in the stock for 5 minutes or until just cooked.

- To serve, arrange the vegetables on a large serving dish or a plate. Working from the center out, top the vegetables with half of the first sauce. Place the fillets of cod on top of the vegetables. Mix the remaining first sauce into the second sauce and pour over the fish. Serve.

Serves 4

RECOMMENDED WINE
White. Pinot Gris, Tocai (Trentino-Alto Adige) Gewurztraminer, Alois Lageder (Trentino-Alto Adige)

MERLUZZO AL VERDUZZO DI CAPRI

COD WITH VERDUZZO DI CAPRI WINE

If you are pressed for time, buy agnolotti from your local pasta shop. I use agnolotti filled with a vegetable. Start with a plate of antipasti of Grilled Zucchini and Eggplant, and Baked Onions.

6	fresh artichoke hearts, sliced	6	1 Tbsp	extra virgin olive oil	15 mL
1¾ lbs	fresh cod, cleaned, scaled and deboned	780 g	2	carrots, finely sliced	2
			2 Tbsp	unsalted butter	25 mL
6	pearl onions, skinned and chopped, plus (see Note)	6		Juice of 1 lemon	
			4	sprigs fresh basil, julienned	4
12	whole pearl onions, skinned	12	12	agnolotti filled with salmon (use	12
	Salt			Lobster Ravioli recipe, (page 76)	
1 tsp	peppercorns	5 mL		and substitute ⅓ lb (150 g)	
1½ cups	white wine, Verduzzo Di Capri or Lacrima Cristi	375 mL		salmon for the lobster)	
1½ cups	fish stock, preferably homemade	375 mL			

RECOMMENDE WINE
White. Frascati, Gotto D'Oro (Lazio)

◞ Preheat an oven to 350°F (180°C).

◞ Clean the artichokes by cutting off the stem at the base and removing the outer leaves until the core becomes visible (the leaves will be a pale green and a cone shape will emerge). Cut enough from the top of the cone that one-quarter of the tender leaves above the heart remain. Cut the artichoke in half vertically. Cut out the fuzzy choke in the center. From the outside of the artichoke heart, pare away remaining tough green parts. Slice the artichoke hearts vertically. Place in water with lemon juice to avoid discoloration. This is not as difficult or time consuming as it sounds.

◞ Butter an oven dish large enough to accommodate the fish. Chop 3 of the pearl onions and sprinkle over the bottom; top with the cod, salt and peppercorns. Add half the wine and half the fish stock. Bake for 10–15 minutes.

◞ Chop 3 more pearl onions. In a separate pan, heat the olive oil and saute the chopped pearl onions, artichoke hearts and carrots. Cook slowly until the vegetables are soft. Add the remaining wine and fish stock and the remaining whole pearl onions. Cook until reduced by one-third. Just prior to finishing, add the butter and lemon juice.

⌁ Drop the agnolotti into boiling salted water and cook until the pasta rises to the surface. Test for doneness. Remove, drain and dress the agnolotti with some of the vegetable sauce. Top with some of the basil.

⌁ Place the cod in a serving dish surrounded by the vegetables and the agnolotti. Top with the remaining sauce. Sprinkle the remaining basil over the entire plate for decoration and serve.

NOTE: *To remove the skins from the pearl onions, cut an "x" in the root end. Plunge the onions into a pot of boiling water. Remove the onions after 30 seconds and run them under cold water. Slice off the root end and the skin will easily come off.*

Serves 4

SALMONE BELLA VISTA

COLD POACHED SALMON WITH MAYONNAISE

Serve the salmon on a buffet with the mayonnaise on the side, grilled vegetables, baked onions, Mozzarella di Bufala and tomato salad and sliced Italian prosciutto.

1	onion, cut in rings or 1 whole green onion	1	6 lbs	whole Atlantic salmon, cleaned and scaled	2¾ kg
1	heart of celery, crushed	1		enough salted water to cover the fish	
4	bay leaves	4			
1 tsp	whole black or green peppercorns	5 mL		FOR THE MAYONNAISE	
1	sprig fresh Italian parsley	1	2	egg yolks	2
1	bunch of fresh dill	1	2 Tbsp	fresh lemon juice	25 mL
1	carrot, sliced	1	1cup	extra virgin olive oil (see Note)	250 mL
3 Tbsp	olive oil	35 mL	¼ tsp	salt	1 mL

RECOMMENDED WINE
For the Cold Salmon – White.
Sauvignon, Collio, Dorigo
(Friuli-Venezia Giulia)
For the Hot Salmon – White.
Fiano di Avellino (Campania)

∾ Place the vegetables, herbs and olive oil in a fish poacher. Wrap the salmon tightly in cheesecloth and place it on top of the vegetables and herbs in the poacher. Cover the salmon with water. Place the fish poacher on the stove and cook over medium to high heat for about 20 minutes. (You can also cook the fish in a preheated oven, at 500°F (260°C) for 45 minutes.) Remove and, if making Cold Salmon, let the fish cool in its stock. When the fish is cool, unwrap it carefully and place it on a serving plate. Carefully remove the skin, except on the head. Remove the eyes and place one cherry or black olive in each eye socket.

∾ To make the mayonnaise, in a food processor, combine the egg yolks with the lemon juice, 3 Tbsp (45 mL) olive oil and salt at high speed for 5 seconds. With the machine running, add the remaining oil, slowly in a continuous flow, until the mayonnaise is thick. Correct for salt and lemon if necessary.

∾ To decorate, place mayonnaise in a pastry bag and decorate the body of the fish creating a scaled design. Place cherries or olives around the plate.

NOTE: *For this recipe a light extra virgin olive oil is required. I have found the best product to use is the Olio Carli by FratelliCarli. This is a delicious oil; the acidity is lower than 0.3%.*

You may also serve the salmon hot with the following delicious sauce. If serving the salmon hot, do not cover the salmon completely with water; cover only the removable plate with 1 inch (25 cm) of salted water. Then cover the fish with aluminum foil and the lid of the poacher and cook in the preheated oven at 500 °F (260 °C) for 45 minutes. Serve the hot salmon with steamed vegetables such as fennel, asparagus and tiny potatoes.

SAUCE WITH CREAM FOR SALMON

¼ cup	unsalted butter	50 mL	1 cup	whipping cream (35%)	250 mL
2 Tbsp	flour	25 mL	1	whole green onion, chopped	1
1 cup	fish stock, preferably homemade	250 mL	10	sprigs fresh dill	10
			1	egg yolk	1
				Salt	

In the top part of a double boiler, melt the butter over hot, gently boiling water. Add the flour, mix and cook for 1 minute. Add the stock and cream and stir. Add the green onion and the dill and cook for 20 minutes. Strain and cool slightly. Add the egg yolk to the sauce and beat it until the yolk is completely amalgamated. Add salt to taste. If necessary, put the sauce back over simmering water until thick. Keep warm until needed.

Serves 8

GRIGLIATA DI PESCE CON SALSA

GRILLED FISH WITH SAUCE

FOR THE SAUCE					
1 cup	mayonnaise	250 mL	1 tsp	chopped fresh mint	5 mL
1 Tbsp	capers	15 mL	2 Tbsp	chopped fresh dill	25 mL
3 Tbsp	grappa, non-aromatic	45 mL	1 tsp	green peppercorns	5 mL
	Pinch of salt		2 lbs	whole or filleted fish (mackerel,	1 kg
1 Tbsp	finely chopped fresh Italian parsley	15 mL		salmon, swordfish or tuna)	

RECOMMENDED WINE
White. Tocai Friulano, G.
Dorigo (Friuli-Venzia Giulia)

- Blend all of the ingredients, except the fish, in a blender or food processor until smooth.
- Grill the fish to taste and serve with the sauce.

Serves 4

CAPESANTE GRIGLIATE

GRILLED SCALLOPS

These grilled fish recipes are simple and delicious.

12	large sea scallops	12	1	clove garlic, crushed	1
4 Tbsp	extra virgin olive oil	60 mL	1 Tbsp	chopped fresh Italian parsley	15 mL
1 Tbsp	red wine vinegar	15 mL	1	lemon	1

Dip scallops in a mixture of 3 Tbsp (45 mL) extra virgin olive oil, red wine vinegar and crushed garlic. Heat a cast iron grill pan until hot and brown the scallops carefully. Do not overcook. Sprinkle with parsley and the remaining extra virgin olive oil. Serve with lemon on the side.

Serves 4

RECOMMENDED WINE
*White. Vintage Tunina,
Jermann (Friuli-Venezia Giulia)
Tocai Friuliano, G. Dorigo
(Friuli-Venezia Giulia)*

GRIGLIATA MISTO

GRILLED SHRIMP, SQUID AND CUTTLEFISH

½ lb	shrimp	250 g		Salt	
½ lb	squid	250 g	2 Tbsp	red wine vinegar	25 mL
½ lb	cuttlefish	250 g	2 Tbsp	chopped fresh Italian parsley	25 mL
5 Tbsp	extra virgin olive oil	70 mL	1	lemon	1
2	cloves garlic, chopped	2			

RECOMMENDED WINE

*White. Vintage Tunina,
Jermann (Friuli-Venezia Giulia)
Tocai Friulano, G. Dorigo
(Friuli-Venezia Giulia)*

꙰ Clean and devein the shrimp and butterfly (gently open to flatten out).

꙰ Clean the squid and cuttlefish and cut into large rings.

꙰ Combine 3 Tbsp (45 mL) extra virgin olive oil, garlic and salt; add the fish and toss to coat.

꙰ Place the shrimp belly side down in a hot cast iron grill pan; add the remaining fish and grill until done, being careful not to overcook. The shrimp should take no more than 1 minute on each side. Before removing the fish, sprinkle with a little red wine vinegar. Remove the fish from the pan with tongs, shaking the fish as you remove it.

꙰ Place the fish in a dish; top with the remaining extra virgin olive oil and a sprinkle of chopped parsley. Serve lemon on the side.

Serves 4

CAPESANTE AL VIN SANTO

SCALLOPS VIN SANTO

Vin Santo (holy wine) is a special, historic wine created to celebrate the mass. This rich sauce goes well with the more subtle taste of Tagliatelle with Herbs to start.

¼ cup	unsalted butter	50 mL		½ cup	Vin Santo, Francescano, dessert	125 mL
12	large sea scallops, cut in half	12			wine	
1 cup	flour	250 mL		½ cup	whipping cream (35%)	125 mL
1¼ cup	fish stock, preferably homemade	285 mL			Salt and pepper	

〜 In a large skillet, heat the butter. Meanwhile, dust the scallops in the flour and shake off excess. Saute the scallops in the hot butter over high heat for about 1 minute until they are brown on both sides. Remove and set aside. Add the fish stock to the skillet, deglaze, and reduce by half. Add the Vin Santo wine and the cream. When the sauce is nearly the desired thickness, add the scallops to coat and warm. Add salt and pepper to taste.

〜 Serve hot with boiled potatoes, rapini and steamed baby carrots, dressed with olive oil and lemon.

Serves 4

RECOMMENDED WINE
White. Vintage Tunina, Jermann (Friuli-Venezia Giulia)
White. Chardonnay Tiefenbrunner (Trentino-Alto Adige)

MEDAGLIONI DI CODA DI ROSPO ALLO ZAFFERANO E CAROTE

MEDALLIONS OF MONKFISH WITH SAFFRON AND CARROT

I love to make this in the summer, the flavor is so delicate and subtle.

3	medium carrots, julienned	3	2 cups	fish stock, preferably homemade	500 mL
½	whole fennel, julienned	½			
1	rib celery, julienned	1	1½ cups	whipping cream (35%)	350 mL
2 Tbsp	unsalted butter	25 mL	1¼ lbs	medallions of monkfish, skinned and cleaned	600 g
12	threads saffron, Turkish if possible	12	1	bunch fresh dill	1
¼ cup	Cognac	50 mL			

RECOMMENDED WINE

White. Rovereto di Gavi, Chiarlo (Piemonte)

~ In a large deep skillet, bring 4 cups (1L) salted water to a boil. Add the vegetables, return to the boil and blanch them for 1 minute. Drain and place them in a bowl of ice water. Remove and pat dry. Saute the vegetables in the butter; add the saffron threads; add the Cognac and flambe. Add ½ cup (125 mL) fish stock and the cream and reduce until lightly thickened. Remove the vegetables with a slotted spoon and place them on a large serving platter. Keep warm.

~ In a large pan, cover the medallions of monkfish with the remaining fish stock and cook over moderate heat for about 7 minutes or until the fish is opaque.

~ Remove the medallions and place them on top of the vegetables on the serving platter.

~ Pour the saffron sauce over the fish.

~ Decorate with dill and serve with plain rice.

Serves 4

PESCE ALLA LIVORNESE

RED SNAPPER, LIVORNO STYLE

Start with a plate of sliced Italian prosciutto and fresh Mozzarella di Bufala, or sliced fresh tomatoes and Mozzarella di Bufala dressed with extra virgin olive oil and chopped fresh basil.

1½ lbs	whole red snappers (4), cleaned	750 g	3 Tbsp	unsalted butter, at room temperature	45 mL
1 Tbsp	extra virgin olive oil	15 mL		Juice of 1 lemon, at room temperature	
	Salt				
3 Tbsp	Dijon mustard, at room temperature	45 mL			

~ Preheat a grill to high.

~ To prepare the fish: Lay the fish on a chopping board and with a sharp knife gently cut into the skin just below the head down the center to the tail (without cutting through the fish); turn the fish over and repeat. Oil the fish on both sides and inside the cavity and sprinkle with salt. Set aside.

~ Mix together the mustard, butter and the lemon juice. Set aside.

~ Place the fish on the grill and cook 6–8 minutes on each side, or until done. Remove to a serving plate and spread with the mustard mixture on both sides. Serve immediately.

Serves 4

RECOMMENDED WINE
White. Cinqueterre (Liguria)
Rosé. Rosato di Bulgheri,
(Antinori)

POULTRY

GALLETTO NERO AL SALE

BLACK CHICKEN WITH ROCK SALT

I had never heard of a "black" chicken but they are readily available at any poultry store and many butchers. Black chickens have a more delicate taste and are juicier and more tender than white chickens. If you don't want to butterfly the chicken yourself, ask the butcher to do it. Rock salt does not absorb liquid; it crystallizes and forms a crust, keeping all the juices inside.

3 lbs	black chicken (or white), or	1.5 kg	4	bay leaves	4
	Cornish hen		2	cloves garlic, thinly sliced	2
8 cups	rock salt or sea salt	2 L		olive oil	
8	fresh sage leaves	8		Peel of ½ a lemon, grated	
1	sprig fresh rosemary	1		Salt	
1	sprig fresh thyme	1			

RECOMMENDED WINE
White. Pinot Grigio (Friuli-Venezia Giulia or Trentino-Alto Adige)

～ Preheat an oven to 500°F (260°C).

～ Clean the chicken; remove the wing tips, neck and feet. Butterfly the chicken (cut along the backbone being careful not to cut all the way through and spread the chicken flat).

～ Lightly oil the bottom of a 12-cup (3 L) roasting pan. Make a base with half the rock salt and lay half the herbs and garlic on top. Moisten the chicken with olive oil, sprinkle with some salt and place it in the pan, skin side up. Place the remaining herbs, garlic and grated lemon on top of the chicken and top with enough rock salt to cover.

～ Bake the chicken for 1 hour. Do not cover. Remove the chicken from the oven, break the salt and serve.

Serves 4

POLLO ALLA DIAVOLA

CHICKEN DIAVOLA

1½ lbs	Cornish hen	750 g			Salt and pepper	
2	cloves garlic	2	⅓ cup	red wine vinegar	75 mL
¼ cup	fresh Italian parsley	50 mL	4	bay leaves	4
⅓ cup	extra virgin olive oil	75 mL				

∾ Butterfly the hen. Trim the bones (remove the spine bones, wing tips, neck and neck fat; remove the ribs and soft breast bone, if desired). Rinse in cold water and pat dry. Set aside.

∾ In a food processor, puree the garlic, parsley and half the olive oil.

∾ Sprinkle the hen with salt and pepper on both sides. Spread the parsley puree over both sides of the hen. In a pan, mix the remaining olive oil and wine vinegar. Dip the hen in the oil/vinegar mixture on both sides. Place 2 bay leaves on a plate and place the hen, breast side up, on the leaves. Top with the other 2 bay leaves. Pour the remaining oil/vinegar mixture over the hen and cover with plastic wrap. Marinate in the refrigerator for a minimum of 1 hour.

∾ Lightly oil the bottom of a cast iron skillet. Heat the skillet until it is very hot. Add the hen to the skillet and place a full pot of water on top of the hen to weight it down. Cook for 5 minutes on each side, or 8 minutes if the hen is large. Serve over mixed baby lettuce leaves with a wedge of lemon and mashed potatoes.

Serves 2

RECOMMENDED WINE
White. Frascati (Lazio) or Fiano di Avellino, Mastroberardino (Campania) Red. Rosso Piceno, Saladini Pilastri (Marche)

POLLO AL FINOCCHIETTO

CHICKEN WITH DILL

This is my favorite roast chicken; it even outdoes my mother's delicious recipe! Start with an appetizer of fresh Mozzarella di Bufala, sliced and sprinkled with a little of the brine from the mozzarella, a drop of extra virgin olive oil and freshly ground pepper.

2¼ lbs	free-range roasting chicken	1 kg	¼ cup	extra virgin olive oil	60 mL
½ cup	salt pork or bacon, finely chopped	125 mL		Salt and pepper	
			1 Tbsp	lemon juice	15 mL
2 Tbsp	fresh dill, finely chopped	25 mL	1	clove garlic, crushed	1
2	cloves garlic, finely chopped	2	2 Tbsp	extra virgin olive oil	25 mL
4	fresh sage leaves, finely chopped	4			

RECOMMENDED WINE

White. Verdicchio (Marche)

~ Preheat an oven to 450°F (230°C).

~ Wash the chicken. Mix the bacon, dill, garlic and sage and stuff the mixture into the cavity. Tie the chicken cavity closed with string, pushing the legs against the body. Moisten the chicken with olive oil and season with salt and pepper.

~ Roast the chicken in a pan for 1 hour, or until the juices run clear when pierced. Remove from the oven.

~ Mix the lemon juice, garlic and oil and serve on the side with the chicken.

Serve with roasted vegetables such as zucchini, eggplant, peppers and potatoes.

Serves 4

POLLO AL LIMONE

CHICKEN WITH LEMON

2¼ lbs	chicken pieces, drumsticks and thighs, skinned	1 kg	1 cup	chicken stock, preferably homemade	250 mL
¼ cup	unsalted butter	50 mL	1	sprig fresh Italian parsley	1
2 Tbsp	olive oil	25 mL		Juice of 1 lemon	
1 cup	dry white wine	250 mL			
	Salt				

~ Wash the chicken and dry with a cloth.

~ In a large skillet, saute the chicken pieces in the butter and olive oil over high heat until golden. Drain off the fat and return the pan to the heat. Add the wine and deglaze; sprinkle with salt and cook until the wine has evaporated. Add the stock and parsley. Cover, reduce the heat to low and cook for 20 minutes or until the chicken juices run clear. Remove the chicken from the pan; pour the lemon juice over the chicken and serve.

Serves 4

MENU SUGGESTION
Serve with mashed potatoes and fresh, steamed asparagus dressed with extra virgin olive oil and lemon; or Risotto with Asparagus (page 79).

RECOMMENDED WINE
White. Fiano di Avellino, Mastroberardino (Campania)

FARAONA IN UMIDO ALLA CONTADINA

GUINEA HEN, FARMER'S STYLE

Start with a plate of prosciutto with fresh figs.

2	cloves garlic	2	4	fresh sage leaves, finely chopped	4
¼ cup	extra virgin olive oil	50 mL	1½ tsp	fresh chopped rosemary	8 mL
1½ lbs	large guinea hen (cut into 8 pieces)	750 g	1 cup	chicken stock, preferably homemade	250 mL
⅓ cup	dry white wine	75 mL		Salt and pepper	
2	fresh tomatoes, or canned tomatoes, finely chopped	2	½ lb	egg noodles, preferably homemade fettuccine	250 g
4	fresh basil leaves, finely chopped	4			

RECOMMENDED WINE

White. Tunina Riserva, Jermann (Friuli-Venezia Giulia) Chardonnay, Lungarotti (Umbria).

◦ In a large pan, lightly brown the garlic in the olive oil; add the Cornish hen pieces and saute for 5 minutes. Add the wine and reduce completely, then add the tomatoes, basil, sage and rosemary and stir. Add the stock and stir. Add salt and pepper. Cover and cook for 40 minutes. Do not let the mixture dry out. Add stock if needed.

◦ Bring a pot of salted water to a boil; add the noodles and half-cook. Drain and add the noodles to the sauce and cook for a few minutes until the pasta is al dente and some of the sauce has absorbed into the noodles. Serve.

Serves 2

CONIGLIO CON OLIVE

RABBIT WITH OLIVES

3½ lbs	rabbit (2 rabbits)	1.5 kg	3	sprigs fresh Italian parsley, chopped	3
⅓ cup	unsalted butter	75 mL		Salt and pepper	
3 Tbsp	olive oil	45 mL	1 cup	tomato sauce	250 mL
1	rib celery, chopped	1	2 cups	chicken stock, preferably homemade	500 mL
1	small onion, chopped	1			
1	carrot, chopped	1	1½ cups	black olives, preferably Gaeta, pitted	375 mL
1	sprig fresh rosemary, chopped	1			
4	bay leaves	4			

∾ Wash and dry the rabbit and cut into pieces.

∾ Place the rabbit pieces in a deep skillet over moderate heat to dry for 1½ minutes. Remove the rabbit. To the skillet, add the butter, olive oil, celery, onion, carrot, and all the herbs; cook for 10 minutes. Add the tomato sauce and the rabbit, sprinkle with salt and pepper, cover and cook over low heat for 1 hour. Add the stock and the olives and cook for 1 more hour. Remove the bay leaves.

∾ Remove the rabbit pieces to a serving platter and keep warm.

∾ Finish the sauce by adding more stock if the sauce is too thick or reducing if it is too thin. Top the rabbit with the sauce. Serve with roasted or mashed potatoes and steamed cauliflower tossed with extra virgin olive oil and lemon.

Serves 6

RECOMMENDED WINE
White. Chardonnay, Lungarotti (Umbria)

RIGATONI CON SPEZZATINO DI POLLO

RIGATONI WITH CHICKEN

Serve with fresh rapini.

4	cloves garlic	4		Salt and pepper	
¼ cup	extra virgin olive oil	50 mL		chopped fresh jalapeno pepper to taste, optional	
4	chicken legs, skinned	4			
4	chicken thighs, skinned	4	8	fresh basil leaves, chopped	8
¾ cup	dry white wine	175 mL	1 lb	rigatoni	500 g
4	ripe, medium tomatoes or 8 canned tomatoes, chopped	4	⅓ cup	grated Pecorino cheese	75 mL
2 cups	chicken stock, preferably homemade	500 mL			

RECOMMENDED WINE

Red. A light red such as Grignolino (Piemonte) or Barbera d'Asti (Piemonte)

~ In a large pan over medium-high heat, saute the garlic in the olive oil until lightly brown. Add the chicken and cook until it is golden on both sides, then add the wine and deglaze the pan. Add the tomatoes and saute for 2 minutes. Add the chicken stock, a little at a time, salt and pepper, jalapeno, if using, and basil. Cover and cook for 25 minutes, adding more stock as needed.

~ Cook the rigatoni in boiling salted water for 10 minutes or until al dente. Drain. Remove the chicken from the pan and keep warm. Place the rigatoni in the pan with the sauce and mix; add half the Pecorino cheese and cook for 30 to 40 seconds until mixed. Place the rigatoni mixture in a serving dish and top with the remaining cheese. Place the chicken next to the rigatoni. Serve warm.

Serves 4

SUPREMA DI POLLO AL VIN SANTO

SUPREME OF CHICKEN VIN SANTO

Serve with a mixture of four vegetables, such as asparagus, fennel, zucchini, mini carrots, green beans, red and white mini potatoes, spinach or rapini.

4	whole skinless boneless chicken breasts	4	1 cup	Vin Santo wine	250 mL
				Salt and pepper to taste	
1½ cups	flour	375 mL	10	sage leaves, chopped	10
1 cup	vegetable oil	250 mL	1 Tbsp	chopped fresh rosemary	15 mL
2 Tbsp	olive oil	25 mL	2	fresh basil leaves, chopped	2
½ cup	unsalted butter	125 mL	2	sprigs fresh Italian parsley, chopped, plus extra for garnish	2
¾ cup	dry white wine	175 mL			
¼ cup	brandy	50 mL			

〜 Cut the whole chicken breasts in half. Wrap each breast in plastic and flatten with a meat cleaver. Lightly flour the chicken. In a large skillet, saute the chicken in the vegetable oil over high heat until golden on both sides. Remove the chicken and reserve. Remove any excess oil from the pan.

〜 To the same pan, add the olive oil and butter and heat on medium. Return the chicken breasts to the pan; add the dry white wine and reduce by half. Add the brandy, Vinsanto wine, salt and pepper and herbs. Cook and turn the breasts at least once until they are coated with the sauce. Place the chicken in a serving dish and top with the sauce. Serve with steamed vegetables of your choice, dressed with extra virgin olive oil and lemon to taste.

Serves 8

MENU SUGGESTION
Start with Pasta with Lentils (Minestra).

RECOMMENDED WINE
White. Verdicchio (Marche)

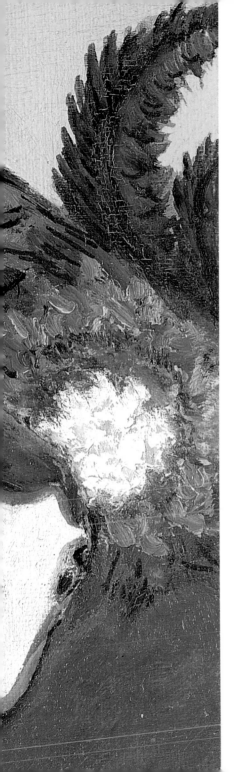

MEATS

FILETTO DI BUE CON GRUVIERA

BEEF FILET WITH GRUYÈRE CHEESE

For a first course, serve Risotto with Radicchio, Eggplant Oriental, Pasta e Fagioli or Pasta with Lentils.

1¾ lbs	filet of beef, fat removed	800 g	1¼ cups	beef stock, preferably	285 mL
2 Tbsp	extra virgin olive oil	25 mL		homemade	
⅓ cup	unsalted butter	75 mL	½ cup	dry Marsala	125 mL
	Salt and pepper		½ cup	dry white wine	125 mL
6–8	slices Gruyère cheese	6–8	1	white truffle, sliced, optional	1

RECOMMENDED WINE

Red. Brunello di Montalcino, Talenti (Toscana)

⁓ Cut the filet into 6 or 8 slices.

⁓ In a large skillet, heat the olive oil and half the butter over high heat and saute the beef slices until they are brown on both sides. Sprinkle the slices with salt and pepper and place them in a baking dish; top with the slices of Gruyère.

⁓ In the same skillet, over high heat, cook the remaining butter and ¼ cup (50 mL) beef stock, Marsala and white wine for 2 to 3 minutes, until the liquid has reduced slightly. If more sauce is needed, add more stock.

⁓ Pour the sauce over the meat; top with the truffle, if using, and serve immediately, with vegtables on the side on a separate plate.

Serves 6–8

BRASATO DI MANZO

BRAISED BEEF

Serve with boiled or mashed potatoes and steamed green beans tossed with extra virgin olive oil, lemon and chopped parsley. Start with Peppers with Bagna Cauda Sauce.

3½ lbs	top sirloin steak	1.5 kg	2	ribs celery, coarsely chopped	2
2 oz	pancetta	50 g	2 Tbsp	dry Marsala	25 mL
2 Tbsp	olive oil	15 mL		Salt and pepper	
2 oz	prosciutto, chopped	50 g	2 cups	beef stock, preferably	500 mL
1	onion, coarsely chopped	1		homemade	
2	carrots, coarsely chopped	2	¼ cup	unsalted butter	50 mL

∼ Pierce the meat at several points with a small, sharp knife and insert small pieces of the pancetta.

∼ In a roasting pan, over medium heat, cook half the olive oil and prosciutto for 2 minutes. Add the onion, carrots, and celery and saute for 5 minutes.

∼ Remove the vegetables and prosciutto and reserve. Raise the heat to high and add the remaining olive oil and the beef and sear. When the meat is brown, add the Marsala, salt and pepper, the reserved vegetables and the prosciutto, and lower the temperature to medium-low. Add stock as needed, ½ cup (125 mL) at a time, to keep the beef from sticking to the pot (use a maximum of 2 cups (500 mL) stock). Braise, covered, for 1½–2 hours or until the meat is tender.

∼ When the meat is done, remove it to a platter. Add the butter to the pan and swirl. If there is too much liquid, reduce. Slice the beef, pour the sauce over it and serve.

Serves 6–8

RECOMMENDED WINE
Red. Barolo (Piemonte)

FILETTO DI MANZO ALLA RICCA

MILLIONAIRE'S FILET OF BEEF

Start with Pasta e Fagioli.

1 lb	sweetbreads, skins removed	500 g	½ cup	Italian prosciutto, diced into	125 g
1 lb	beef filet, fat removed	500 g		½-inch (1 cm) cubes	
1 Tbsp	flour	15 mL	½ cup	beef stock, preferably	125 mL
¼ cup	unsalted butter	50 mL		homemade	
¼ cup	extra virgin olive oil	50 mL	1	medium white or black truffle,	1
	Salt			sliced, optional	

RECOMMENDED WINE
Red. Barolo (Piemonte)

∽ Boil the sweetbreads in water for about 30 minutes. Cool, slice and set aside.

∽ Cut the beef into ½-inch (1 cm) slices and sprinkle the slices with the flour. In a large skillet, heat the butter and olive oil over high heat and saute the filets until golden on both sides; reduce the heat. Salt the filets lightly. Place the sweetbreads and the prosciutto on top of the filets. Add the beef stock and cook over moderate heat until the meat is cooked to your preference and the stock is reduced by half. (If the stock is not thick enough, continue to reduce after removing the meat.) Remove the slices of beef to a serving plate. Pour the sauce over the beef. Top with the sliced truffle, if using, and serve.

Serves 4

STUFATO AL BAROLO

PRIME RIB WITH BAROLO

Even though it is odd to cook a prime rib roast this long in North America, this is the approach required to achieve peak flavor and the proper texture of this delicious sauce. It is the main event in this recipe.

3½ lbs	prime rib of beef, deboned	1.5 kg	1	bottle Barolo or Cabernet	1
1	carrot, cut in 1-inch (2.5 cm) pieces	1		Sauvignon wine	
			¼ cup	unsalted butter	50 mL
2	ribs celery, crushed	2	1	onion, coarsely chopped	1
1	3-inch cinnamon stick	1		Salt and pepper	
5	whole cloves	5			

∼ Place the roast in a deep casserole with the carrot, celery, cinnamon and cloves; cover with the wine and marinate for 24 hours.

∼ Preheat an oven to 450°F (230°C).

∼ Remove the meat from the marinade and pat dry. In a roasting pan, melt the butter over medium heat and saute the onion. Increase the heat to high, add the meat and brown on all sides. Add the marinade with the vegetables, but remove the cinnamon stick. Cover and roast for 4 hours. Remove the roast and strain the juices and vegetables. If the sauce is too thick, add some beef stock or water.

∼ Slice the meat and serve with the sauce.

Serves 6

MENU SUGGESTION
Serve with boiled potatoes and french cut green beans. Start with a soup (Puree of Squash); or a salad.

RECOMMENDED WINES
Red. Barolo (Piemonte); Tignanello, Antinori (Toscana); Chianti Classico, Badia a Passignano, Antinori (Toscana)

SELLA D'AGNELLO ARROSTO

CROWN ROAST OF LAMB

Serve with Potato Gateau and boiled fennel dressed with extra virgin olive oil and lemon.

1	whole rack of lamb, fully trimmed	1	1	rib celery, crushed	1
	Olive oil		1	sprig fresh rosemary, needles only	1
	Salt and pepper				
1 Tbsp	olive oil	15 mL	½ cup	dry white wine	125 mL
1	carrot, coarsely chopped	1	1	sprig fresh mint, plus extra leaves for garnish	1
1	onion, coarsely chopped	1			

RECOMMENDED WINE

*Red. Barolo, Einaudi
(Piemonte)
Barbaresco, 'Asili', Produttori
del Barbaresco (Piemonte)*

〜 Preheat an oven to 500°F (260°C).

〜 Cover the ends of the individual lamb ribs with foil. Drizzle the lamb lightly with olive oil and sprinkle with salt and pepper. Place the meat in a roasting pan.

〜 In a skillet, heat the olive oil and saute the vegetables and rosemary until cooked. Put the mixture in the roasting pan around the meat. Place the pan on the middle rack of the preheated oven and cook for 20 minutes for medium rare, or 25 minutes for medium.

〜 Remove the meat from the pan. Add the wine and the mint and deglaze the pan over high heat. Strain the sauce, being careful to remove as much of the fat as possible. Slice the roast and serve with the sauce. Garnish with mint leaves.

Serves 4

COSCIA D'AGNELLO

LEG OF LAMB

This is an elegant presentation for a special dinner with a delicious medley of flavors.

1	whole leg of lamb, upper half deboned; lower half with shank	1	1½ cups	vegetable oil	375 mL
			1	carrot, coarsely chopped	1
3	cloves garlic, thinly sliced	3	2	ribs celery, crushed	2
12	fresh sage leaves	12	1	medium onion, quartered	1
4	sprigs fresh rosemary	4	4	sprigs fresh thyme	4
2 Tbsp	green peppercorns	25 mL	¼ cup	red wine vinegar	50 mL
½ cup	olive oil	125 mL	1 cup	dry white wine	250 mL
	Salt and pepper		8	fresh mint leaves	8

∽ Preheat an oven to 500°F (260°C).

∽ Open the top part of the leg of lamb and stuff with the garlic, 6 sage leaves, 1 sprig of rosemary, and half the green peppercorns. Tie the meat tightly with butcher's string. Moisten the outside of the lamb with half the olive oil and sprinkle with salt and pepper.

∽ In a large frying pan, heat the vegetable oil and brown the leg of lamb on all sides. Place the lamb in a roasting pan with the remaining olive oil and add the carrot, celery, onion, 1 sprig rosemary, 2 sprigs thyme and the red wine vinegar. Roast the lamb, covered, for 30 minutes for medium rare or 45 minutes for medium.

∽ Remove the lamb from the pan and keep warm. Deglaze the pan with the wine, then add the remaining herbs (rosemary, sage, mint). Remove any excess oil with a spoon and strain the sauce. Add the remaining green peppercorns. Slice the leg of lamb from the front to bottom of the shank. Top with the sauce and serve.

Serves 6

RECOMMENDED WINE
*Red. Schioppettino, G. Dorigo (Friuli-Venezia Giulia)
Chianti Classico Riserva, Villa Antinori (Toscana)*

COSCIOTTO D'AGNELLO ARROSTO

ROASTED LEG OF LAMB WITH HERBS

This is a regional dish from Lazio. Serve with Roasted Potatoes with Goosefat and Rapini. Start with Grilled Mushrooms or Artichokes with Wild Herbs from the Countryside.

1	whole leg of fresh lamb, center bone removed	1	1½ cups	vegetable oil Salt and pepper	375 mL
3	sprigs fresh rosemary	3	1	carrot, quartered	1
10	fresh sage leaves	10	1	rib celery, crushed	1
6	cloves garlic, crushed	6	¾ cup	dry white wine	175 mL

RECOMMENDED WINE

Red. Sassicaia (Toscana)
Cabernet Terre di Franciacorte
(Lombardia)

∽ Preheat an oven to 450°F (230°C).

∽ Open up the leg of lamb and stuff with 1 sprig rosemary, 4 sage leaves, and 3 cloves of garlic. Close the leg and tie tightly with butcher's string. Coat the outside of the lamb with some of the vegetable oil. Sprinkle with salt and pepper.

∽ In a large skillet, heat the remaining vegetable oil over high heat and brown the leg of lamb on all sides. Remove and place the lamb in a roasting pan with the carrot, celery, remaining garlic and 1 sprig of rosemary. Roast for 45 minutes for medium rare.

∽ Remove the meat from the pan and add the white wine, the remaining rosemary and sage leaves and deglaze the pan over high heat (this last process is important to release the flavors from the herbs). Strain the sauce and pour over the sliced lamb.

Serves 6

SELLA DI MAIALE ARROSTO

ROAST PORK LOIN

I prefer to use pork shoulder, sometimes called Boston butt, because it is juicier and tastier. Serve with polenta, chicory or rapini.

3½ lbs	boneless, tied, pork loin	1.5 kg	2	ribs celery, cut lengthwise	2
6	garlic cloves, cut in half	6	1	carrot, cut lengthwise	1
½ cup	extra virgin olive oil	125 mL	1	onion, quartered	1
¼ cup	vegetable oil	50 mL	1 cup	dry red wine	250 mL
2 Tbsp	salt	25 mL	8	bay leaves	8
2 Tbsp	whole black peppercorns, ground	25 mL	1	sprig fresh rosemary	1
			8	large, fresh sage leaves	8

∽ Preheat an oven to 400°F (200°C)

∽ Cut shallow slits in the meat with a sharp-pointed knife. Insert the garlic in the slits. In a roasting pan, combine half the olive oil with the vegetable oil. Moisten the outside of the roast with half of the mixed oils. Combine the salt and pepper and roll the roast in the mixture.

∽ Heat the remaining mixed oils in the pan and when hot, add the meat and brown on all sides. Remove the meat from the pan and discard the heated oil.

∽ Wipe the pan clean and add the remaining olive oil, meat, celery, carrot and onion. Return the roasting pan to the heat on the stove and when hot, add the wine and reduce by three-quarters; add the bay leaves, rosemary and sage. Cover the pan with a lid or foil and bake for 1 hour.

∽ Remove the roast from the oven. Place the meat on a serving platter and slice to desired thickness. Strain the remaining juices in the pan and serve.

Serves 4

RECOMMENDED WINE
Red. Barbera d'Alba, Luigi Einaudi (Piemonte)

SPALLA DI MAIALE ARROSTO

ROAST SHOULDER OF PORK

Serve with roasted potatoes with goosefat, roasted red peppers and rapini.

4	garlic cloves, chopped	4	¼ cup	extra virgin olive oil	50 mL
8	large sage leaves	8		Salt	
2 Tbsp	fresh rosemary leaves	25 mL	3 cups	whole milk	750 mL
6	bay leaves	6	1 cup	water	250 mL
6 lbs	boneless, tied shoulder of pork	3 kg			

RECOMMENDED WINE
White. Ribolla Gialla, G. Dorigo (Friuli-Venezia Giulia)

~ Mix the garlic, sage, rosemary and 4 bay leaves. Moisten the meat with 2 Tbsp (25 mL) olive oil and massage it with the garlic and herb mixture. Place the meat in a deep dish and refrigerate for 2 days; massage the meat at least once a day to work in the herbs.

~ Preheat an oven to 400°F (200°C).

~ In a roasting pan, place the remaining olive oil, bay leaves and meat. Sprinkle with salt; add the milk and water. Place the roast in the preheated oven, uncovered, and roast for 2 hours (20 minutes per pound).

~ Remove the roast from the oven, place on a serving platter and slice. Reduce the milk, if necessary, until it is thickened. Strain the liquid and pour over the sliced meat.

Serves 8

MEDAGLIONI DI VITELLO ALLA SALVIA

MEDALLIONS OF VEAL WITH SAGE

Serve with asparagus and start with Tagliatelle with Herbs.

1¼ lbs	whole filet of veal	600 g		Salt and pepper	
½ cup	unsalted butter	125 mL	8	fresh sage leaves	8
¼ cup	extra virgin olive oil	50 mL	1 Tbsp	chopped fresh Italian parsley,	15 mL
½ cup	dry white wine	125 mL		prezzemolo strizzato (see Note)	

Cut the fillet of veal into 8 equal rounds. In a large skillet, heat one-third of the butter and all of the olive oil and saute the veal medallions on both sides until they are golden. Remove the veal from the pan and discard the butter and oil. Return the veal to the pan and, over high heat, deglaze with the wine. Add the remaining butter, salt and pepper, sage leaves and stir for 30 seconds (the flavor will be released from the sage leaves). Remove the medallions from the heat to a serving plate and top with the sauce and the prezzemolo strizzato.

NOTE: *Prezzemolo strizzato is a process of preparing parsley that will be used solely for decoration. It removes the flavor from the parsley, leaving the green leaves for decoration. Chop the parsley finely then place it in a towel and twirl the towel until it forms a ball. Place the "ball" of parsley under cold water, let the water run, then squeeze the towel until the parsley is dry.*

Serves 4

RECOMMENDED WINE
Light Red. Barbera d'Alba, Luigi Einaudi (Piemonte)
White. Pinot Grigio (Friuli-Venezia Giulia or Trentino-Alto Adige)

VITELLO PICCATA AL PREZZEMOLE

VEAL WITH LEMON AND PARSLEY

For a first course, serve Risotto with Scampi.

1¾ lbs	filet of veal	800 g	4	bay leaves	4
1 cup	flour	250 mL	8	fresh sage leaves	8
½ cup	unsalted butter	125 mL	2 Tbsp	fresh Italian parsley, finely chopped	25 mL
½ cup	olive oil	125 mL			
½ cup	dry white wine	125 mL		Juice of 1 lemon	

RECOMMENDED WINE
White. Ribolla Gialla, G. Dorigo (Friuli-Venezia Giulia)

〜 Cut the veal into ¼-inch (.6 cm) slices and flatten with a meat cleaver or a meat tenderizer. Dredge the veal slices in flour.

〜 In a large skillet, heat half the butter and the olive oil. Saute the veal slices over high heat until brown on both sides. Remove the meat from the pan and discard the butter and oil. Return the meat to the pan, add the wine and reduce by half. Add the remaining butter, bay and sage leaves and lemon juice. Add half the parsley and cook about 20 seconds more. Remove the bay leaves and sage before serving.

〜 Place the veal on a large serving plate, top with the sauce and the remaining parsley and serve.

Serves 8

SCALOPPINE CON FUNGHI DI BOSCO

VEAL SCALLOPS WITH WILD MUSHROOMS

Serve with Pureed Potatoes and Carrots.

1 lb	filet of veal	500 g	2	sprigs fresh thyme, leaves only	2
¼ cup	extra virgin olive oil	50 mL	1 Tbsp	chopped fresh Italian parsley	15 mL
1	white onion, or small cooking onion, finely chopped	1	¾ cup	beef or chicken stock, preferably homemade	175 mL
1 lb	mixed mushrooms (oyster, portobello, chanterelle, porcini, if available), cleaned and thinly sliced	500 g	1 cup	white flour	250 mL
			¾ cup	vegetable oil	175 mL
			¼ cup	unsalted butter	50 mL
			½ cup	whipping cream (35%)	125 mL
½ cup	dry white wine	125 mL		Salt and pepper	
4	fresh sage leaves	4			

➤ Slice the veal into 8 pieces and pound until thin. Set aside.

➤ In a large skillet, heat the olive oil, then add the onions and saute them until they are translucent. Increase the heat to high, add the sliced mushrooms and cook for 2 minutes. Add the wine, sage, 1 sprig thyme and parsley. Reduce the wine by half and add the stock. Cook for 4 minutes.

➤ Dredge the veal slices in the flour. In a large skillet, heat the vegetable oil and saute the meat over high heat until golden on both sides. Remove the meat.

➤ Add the cooked scallops of veal and the butter to the mushroom sauce. Stir until the meat is warm and mixed with the mushrooms. Add the cream and cook for 2 minutes until the sauce thickens slightly.

➤ Place the meat on a serving plate and top with the mushroom sauce. Sprinkle with the remaining thyme.

Serves 4

RECOMMENDED WINE
Light Red. Grignolino (Piemonte)

FEGATO DI VITELLO CON SALVIA

PROVIMI VEAL LIVER WITH SAGE

2 cups	white pearl onions, skinned	500 mL	12	fresh sage leaves	12
1¼ lbs	provimi veal liver	600 g	½ cup	dry white wine	125 mL
1 cup	flour	250 mL		Salt and pepper	
½ cup	unsalted butter	125 mL	12	new white potatoes	12

RECOMMENDED WINE

*Rosé. Rosato di Bolgheri,
Antinori (Toscana)*

~ Cut an "x" in the root end of the onions and plunge the onions into a pot of boiling water. Remove after 30 seconds and run under cold water. Slice off the root end and slip off the skins. Saute the onions in olive oil until tender-crisp and set aside.

~ Rinse the liver and pat it dry. Just before cooking, dust the liver slices with the flour; shake off the excess.

~ Cook the potatoes in boiling salted water for 15 minutes, or until tender.

~ In a large skillet, melt the butter over medium-high heat. Add half the sage leaves and cook them until they wilt. Add the liver and cook for 1 minute on each side. Remove the liver and place in a serving dish. Add the wine to the skillet with the remaining sage leaves and reduce by two-thirds. Pour the sauce over the liver and serve with the potatoes and pearl onions.

Serves 6

RACK OF CARIBOU

Caribou and venison are both wild meats, yet different in taste. Caribou is a larger animal with a more gentle taste and tender, very dark meat. Since caribou is still a wild animal, as opposed to the cultivated venison, quotas are controlled by the Canadian government. This is a recipe primarily for hunters, but if you are enterprising, you can order the meat from a restaurant food supplier. As an alternative, use venison or beef tenderloin.

3 Tbsp	olive oil	45 mL	¾ cup	homemade caribou stock	175 mL
½	medium onion, thinly sliced	½		(recipe follows) or beef stock	
1 lb	mixed, fresh mushrooms	500 g	4	fresh sage leaves	4
	(portobello, porcini, shiitake,		2 Tbsp	unsalted butter	25 mL
	chanterelle), thinly sliced			Salt and pepper	
½ cup	dry red wine	125 mL	1	whole rack of caribou	1
1 Tbsp	pine nuts	15 mL			

〜 Preheat a broiler.

〜 In a large skillet, heat 2 Tbsp (25 mL) of olive oil and saute the onion until translucent. Add the mushrooms and stir continuously until they are thoroughly mixed with the onions. Add the wine and pine nuts and reduce by three-quarters. Add the stock and sage and reduce the liquid by half. Add the butter, salt and pepper.

〜 Oil the rack of caribou (or beef tenderloin) with the remaining olive oil. Sprinkle with salt and pepper. Place the meat in the oven on the middle rack and broil for 20 minutes for medium rare. When cooked, cut the caribou into single or double chops.

〜 Pool the mushroom sauce on a platter and top with the chops. Decorate the serving plate with a colored maple leaf, if you like.

Serves 4

CARIBOU STOCK

1	onion, thinly sliced	1	3 Tbsp	olive oil	45 mL
	Trimmings from the rack (or ask		2	cloves garlic, sliced or crushed	2
	the butcher for the trimmings		1 cup	water	250 mL
	(gristle, bones, meat)		3	sprigs fresh Italian parsley	3
1½	ribs celery, crushed	1½	1	sprig fresh rosemary	1
2	carrots, coarsely chopped	2		Salt	
½ cup	flour	125 mL			

MENU SUGGESTION

*For a first course, serve smoked
salmon or sturgeon with capers.
For the main course, serve
polenta and grilled radicchio
with the caribou.*

RECOMMENDED WINE

*Red. Sassicaia (Tuscany)
Cabernet Sauvignon, Maculan
(Veneto)
Cabernet Sauvignon,
Mormoreto, Frescobaldi
(Toscana)*

~ In a hot cast iron skillet, burn half the onion. Remove and set aside.

~ Dredge the meat trimmings, celery and carrots in the flour. In a large skillet, heat the olive oil and saute the garlic, meat trimmings, remaining onion and vegetables until brown. Add the water, burnt onion, parsley and rosemary and simmer for 1 hour. Add more water if necessary. Add salt to taste at end of cooking. Strain and return to the pan; reduce until slightly thickened.

Yield: ¾ cup (175mL)

RACK OF VENISON

1	whole rack of venison	1		2	dried apricots, sliced	2
2 Tbsp	olive oil	25 mL		1	dried fig, sliced	1
2 tsp	unsalted butter	10 mL		2	fresh sage leaves	2
1 cup	dry red wine	250 mL			Salt and pepper	
2 Tbsp	mixed dried berries	25 mL			Watercress for garnish	
	(cranberries, blackberries,					
	raisins)					

⌁ Preheat a broiler.

⌁ Oil the rack of venison with 1 Tbsp (15 mL) of the olive oil. Broil for 20–30 minutes for medium rare.

⌁ In a large skillet, heat the butter, the remaining olive oil, wine, dried berries, apricots, figs and sage. Cook until reduced by half. Take the skillet off the heat and keep the sauce warm.

⌁ When the meat is cooked, reheat the sauce, add the meat and mix until it is well coated (about 2 minutes). Remove and slice the meat into chops.

⌁ Pool the remaining sauce on a serving plate and top with the meat. Garnish with watercress and serve immediately with Puree of Chestnuts (page 142) on the side.

⌁ This sauce would also be delicious with a loin of pork. Start with Puree of Squash Soup or Pasta with Beans. Serve the venison with grilled radicchio and polenta.

Serves 4

RECOMMENDED WINE
Red. Cabernet Sauvignon, Mormoreto, Frescobaldi (Toscana)

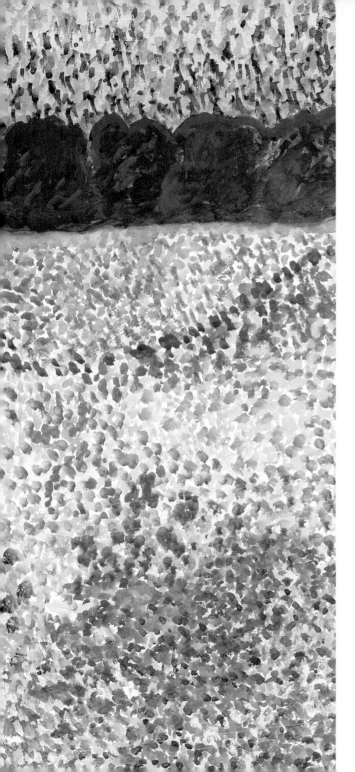

VEGETABLES AND SIDE DISHES

ASPARAGI

ASPARAGUS

	Fresh bunch of asparagus spears		grated Parmigiano Reggiano cheese
2 Tbsp	butter	30mL	

﹏ Preheat a broiler.

﹏ Snap the hard ends off the asparagus. Tie the asparagus spears together with an elastic band, or string, and boil in salted water for 1 minute. Remove. Alternately, steam the asparagus in the microwave until al dente.

﹏ Coat a shallow baking dish with melted butter and place the asparagus in the dish. Top the asparagus with grated Parmigiano Reggiano cheese and broil until the cheese is melted and lightly browned. Serve.

Serve 4–6 spears per person

BARBABIETOLE (DA ZUCCHERO)

BEETS

Serve for a light summer lunch with freshly baked bread, Desalted Anchovies (page 44), fresh Mozzarella di Bufala and olives.

6	beets, small-to-medium, washed and unpeeled	6	2 Tbsp	extra virgin olive oil	25 mL
3 Tbsp	capers	45 mL		Red wine vinegar, to taste	
2	medium sweet onions, thinly sliced	2		Salt and pepper	

- Remove the beet tops and reserve for another use.

- In a large saucepan, bring salted water to a boil. Add the beets and cook over medium heat for 30 minutes or until the beets are cooked al dente.

- Drain the beets; cool, peel and slice them.

- Place the beet slices on a serving plate and top with capers and onions. Sprinkle with olive oil, red wine vinegar, salt and pepper.

Serves 4

ZUCCHINE FRITTE ALL' ACETO E ERBE

FRIED ZUCCHINI WITH WINE VINEGAR AND HERBS

¾ cup	vegetable oil	175 mL	3	cloves garlic, finely sliced	3
¾ cup	extra virgin olive oil	175 mL	2 Tbsp	chopped fresh mint, plus extra for garnish	25 mL
6	medium zucchini, washed and sliced into rounds	6	1 Tbsp	finely chopped fresh Italian parsley	15 mL
2 cups	white flour	500 mL			
2	eggs, well beaten with ¼ cup (50 mL) milk	2	2 tsp	finely chopped fresh dill, plus extra for garnish	8 mL
½ cup	red wine vinegar	125 mL		Salt	

⌐ In a skillet, heat the vegetable oil and ¼ cup (50 mL) of the olive oil until hot (the olive oil tempers the taste of the vegetable oil). Dip the sliced zucchini in the flour, then the egg, then the flour again. Shake off the excess flour. Fry quickly in the hot oil for about 1 minute. Remove and drain the zucchini on paper towels.

⌐ Mix the remaining olive oil, vinegar, garlic and herbs to make a vinaigrette.

⌐ Layer the zucchini on a flat serving plate. Sprinkle with salt and some of the vinaigrette. Repeat. Let the zucchini marinate for 1 hour before serving. Decorate the plate with sprigs of mint and dill.

Serves 6

FUNGHI ALLA GRIGLIA

GRILLED MUSHROOMS

Serve with grilled or roasted meat.

8	Portobello mushrooms, 5 inches in (12.5 cm) diameter	8	Extra virgin olive oil
			Salt

~ Remove the stems from the mushrooms. Wipe the mushroom caps with a damp cloth. Sprinkle the mushrooms with a little olive oil and salt.

~ Grill the mushrooms on a hot cast iron skillet; add more oil if needed. Remove when cooked to taste.

Serves 4

RADICCHIO TREVISANO GRIGLIATO

GRILLED TREVISO RADICCHIO

4	bunches radicchio, Treviso, if	4		Salt	
	available		1	lemon	1
	Extra virgin olive oil				

❧ Wash and dry the radicchio. Slice the radicchio lengthwise in quarters (without cutting off the bottom which will hold the leaves together). Gently toss with olive oil and salt.

❧ Grill the radicchio on a hot cast iron grill pan until they are wilted and lightly brown. Remove. Put the radicchio on a plate and dress with extra virgin olive oil and lemon juice.

Serves 4

POLENTA

Serve with any game meat including venison and caribou.

8 cups	cold water	2 L	1	sprig rosemary	1
1 tsp	salt	5 mL	2 Tbsp	extra virgin olive oil	25 mL
6	sage leaves	6	2 cups	coarse cornmeal	500 mL

In a heavy saucepan, bring the water, salt, herbs and olive oil to a boil. Remove the herbs after a few minutes (once they have released their flavor). Reduce the heat to low. Add the cornmeal, a little at a time, and cook, stirring continuously with a wooden spoon until the mixture is thickened, about 30 minutes. Add more water if necessary.

Remove the polenta from the heat and let it rest for a few minutes. Spoon the polenta into a shallow baking dish and let it sit until it becomes firm. Cut into servings.

Serve as is or grill in a hot cast iron pan.

Serves 6

SFORMATO DI PATATE

POTATO GATEAU

4	large white potatoes, unpeeled	4	2 Tbsp	coarsely chopped fresh Italian parsley	25 mL
1	egg	1	¼ cup	unsalted butter, melted	50 mL
½ cup	grated Parmigiano Reggiano cheese	125 mL		Salt and pepper to taste	

~ Preheat an oven to 350°F (180°C).

~ Cook the potatoes in boiling salted water until done, about 30 minutes. Peel. Press the potatoes through a potato ricer. Add the egg, half the cheese, and all of the parsley and butter; mix well. Add salt and pepper.

~ Butter a gratin dish. Add the potatoes; sprinkle with the remaining cheese and bake, uncovered, until the potatoes are brown on top, 10–15 minutes.

Serves 4–6

PUREA DI PATATE

PUREED POTATOES

This is a different way to prepare potatoes. It is light and fluffy and delicious.

4	large potatoes, preferably Yukon Gold	4	2 Tbsp	chopped fresh Italian parsley	25 mL
				Salt and pepper	
2	cloves garlic, crushed	2	⅓ cup	extra virgin olive oil	75 mL

~ Wash the potatoes and boil them with their skins on. When they are cooked after about 30 minutes, drain, reserving one ladle of the potato water. Cool slightly, peel and pass through a potato ricer or a foodmill. If the potatoes are too dry, add some of the potato water.

~ Add the garlic, parsley, salt and pepper and extra virgin olive oil. Mix and serve.

NOTE: *For a variation, add 3 medium carrots; cook with the potatoes and proceed as above.*

Serves 4–6

PUREA DI CASTAGNE

PUREE OF CHESTNUTS

Serve with wild meats such as venison, caribou or other game. If you are less adventurous, serve with a filet of beef. The chestnut puree can also be served on sliced or grilled polenta.

2¼ lbs	fresh Italian chestnuts or 2	1 kg	¼ cup	unsalted butter	50 mL
	10-oz (284 mL) cans, whole		2 Tbsp	extra virgin olive oil	25 mL
	peeled chestnuts		½ cup	whipping cream (35%)	125 mL
5	bay leaves	5	1	egg yolk	1
½	small white onion, finely chopped	½		Salt and pepper	

~ If using fresh chestnuts: Wash the nuts in cold water, then soak them in warm water for 20 minutes. Drain. Place the nuts, flat side down, on a board and make a horizontal cut down the center of the nut, without cutting into the chestnut meat; do not cut the flat side. Boil the softened, cut chestnuts and bay leaves in a pot with water to cover for approximately 20 minutes. When the chestnuts are soft, drain, reserving the water. Cool slightly. Peel while the nuts are warm, making sure to remove the outer and inner skin.

~ If using canned chestnuts: Drain the chestnuts, reserving the liquid. Rinse in cold water.

~ Saute the onion in half the butter and the olive oil until it is transparent. Cut the chestnuts in small pieces and add them to the onions; cook for 3–4 minutes. Add 1 cup (250 mL) of the chestnut water (or reserved liquid from the can) and continue cooking for 2 minutes. Blend the mixture in a food processor. Return to the pot and bring to a boil. Mix the cream and egg yolk together. To the pot, add the remaining butter, cream and egg yolk mixture, and mix quickly until the chestnut puree is slightly thick. Add salt and pepper.

NOTE: *Fresh chestnuts are readily available in the fall. Canned chestnuts can be found at gourmet food shops or Italian specialty shops.*

Serves 6

BROCCOLI RABE

RAPINI

This method of cooking rapini provides quality taste with less fat.

1	bunch rapini	1	2 Tbsp	extra virgin olive oil	25 mL
4	cloves garlic,crushed	4			

∾ Remove and discard the thick stems and old, hard leaves of the rapini.

∾ In a small saucepan, fry the garlic in the olive oil until it is lightly brown.

∾ In a large pot, bring salted water to a boil, add the rapini and the olive oil/garlic mixture and cook until the rapini is al dente. Drain the rapini and serve immediately.

Serves 4

PEPERONI ARROSTO

ROASTED PEPPERS

I like roasting the peppers on top of the stove in a grill pan because the peppers do not overcook and they remain firm. When I have roasted them under a broiler in the oven, they are often overcooked and mushy.

4	red bell peppers	4	1 Tbsp	chopped fresh Italian parsley	15 mL
1	clove garlic, crushed	1		Salt	
3 Tbsp	extra virgin olive oil	45 mL			

~ Wash and dry the peppers. Place them on a very hot cast iron grill pan and cook until the skin is black on all sides. Be careful not to overcook, the flesh should be firm. Place the peppers in a paper bag for 15 minutes. When cool, remove the blackened peel; it will come off easily.

~ Remove the seeds, inner pulp and core. Do not rinse the peppers. Cut the peppers in strips and place them in a bowl. Add the garlic, olive oil, parsley and a little salt; toss. Let the peppers marinate for at least 1 hour. Just before serving, remove the garlic clove. Roasted peppers should be served at room temperature.

NOTE: *Roasted peppers can be frozen in plastic bags, either dressed or undressed, in small portions.*

Serves 8

PATATE ARROSTO AL GRASSO D'OCA

ROASTED POTATOES WITH GOOSEFAT

1 lb	large red potatoes	500 g	2	cloves garlic, crushed	2
	Salt and pepper		2 Tbsp	goosefat, melted	25 mL
1 Tbsp	chopped fresh rosemary	15 mL			

~ Preheat an oven to 450°F (230°C).

~ Cut the potatoes into large dice. Blanch them in boiling salted water for 3–4 minutes. Drain.

~ Put the potatoes in a roasting pan and sprinkle with salt and pepper, rosemary, garlic, and the melted goosefat. Bake in the oven until the potatoes are golden brown, about 30 minutes, turning once or twice during cooking.

NOTE: *Canned goosefat can be found at speciality food stores, but why not roast a goose and retain the fat?*

Serves 4

CICORIA SALTATA

SAUTEED CHICORY

Chicory is another Italian vegetable, like arugula and radicchio, that has become available in North America. It has long, slender, dark green leaves with white stalks and a refreshing taste.

1 lb	baby chicory or baby dandelion leaves	500 g	3	cloves garlic, sliced	3
3 Tbsp	extra virgin olive oil	45 mL	1 Tbsp	red wine vinegar	15 mL

~ Remove the chicory root and wash the leaves in cold water.

~ In a large pot, parboil the leaves in salted water. Drain. Squeeze the liquid out by hand or in a cloth towel.

~ Heat the olive oil and saute the garlic until it is light brown. Add the leaves and saute for 3 minutes. In the last minute, add the vinegar and toss. Serve.

Serves 4

BIETA SVIZZERA CON PARMIGIANO

SWISS CHARD, PARMIGIANO STYLE

Serve as a side dish with fresh pepper.

2	bunches Swiss chard	2			Salt	
4	large fresh tomatoes	4	1 cup		grated Parmigiano Reggiano	250 mL
1	onion, thinly sliced	1			cheese	
12	fresh basil leaves	12				

∾ Preheat an oven to 350°F (180°C).

∾ Wash the Swiss chard. Remove the green tops from the stems and cut them into large julienne. Reserve.

∾ Cut 2 inches (25 cm) off the stems (from the bottom of the green tops) and discard the rest.

∾ Butter an oven dish and arrange the Swiss chard stems over the bottom. Layer with the tomato, onion, reserved green tops, basil, a sprinkle of salt and cheese. Repeat layers, ending with the remaining cheese. Cover and bake for 25 minutes; uncover and bake an additional 20 minutes.

NOTE: *Shreaded mozzarella can also be added with the Parmesan cheese.*

Serves 6

DESSERTS

BISCOTTI ALLA PASTA DI MANDORLE

ALMOND COOKIES

12 oz	whole almonds with skins	375 g	½ cup	pure almond paste (best quality)	125 mL
¾ cup	granulated sugar	175 mL	½ cup	egg white (3–4 egg whites)	125 mL
1 tsp	natural almond extract	5 mL			

〜 Preheat an oven to 350°F (180°C).

〜 Blend all the ingredients in a food processor, except the egg whites, until the mixture is crumbly. Add egg whites and mix until just combined.

〜 Drop by teaspoonfuls (5 mL) 1 inch (2.5 cm) apart onto a well greased cookie sheet.

〜 Bake for 15 to 20 minutes, or until lightly browned.

Yield: 40 cookies

TORTA MOCA E MANDORLE

ALMOND MOCHA TORTE

7 oz	whole almonds with skins, finely ground	200 g
⅓ cup	finely ground dry espresso beans	75 mL
2½ Tbsp	unsweetened cocoa powder	30 mL
8	large eggs, separated	8
¾ cup	granulated sugar	175 mL

FOR THE MOCHA FILLING

3½ cups	whipping cream (35%)	750 mL
6 oz	semisweet chocolate, cut in small pieces	175 g
6 Tbsp	dry instant coffee	75 mL
4 Tbsp	granulated sugar	50 mL
6 Tbsp	espresso coffee	75 mL
2 Tbsp	brandy	25 mL

～ Preheat an oven to 350°F (180°C).

～ Put the almonds, espresso and cocoa in a bowl and stir until mixed. Set aside.

～ Beat the egg whites until foamy. Slowly add the sugar and continue to beat until the whites are almost stiff. Set aside.

～ Beat the egg yolks until thick and lemon yellow; gently fold in the egg whites; add the almond mixture and gently fold until just mixed.

～ Pour the mixture into four 9-inch (23 cm) cake pans, ungreased and lined with waxed paper.

～ Bake for 25 to 30 minutes. Remove from the oven and let cool completely in the pans.

～ In a heavy pot, over high heat, bring the cream to a boil; add the chocolate, instant coffee and sugar; stir until completely dissolved. Remove from the heat and place the mixture in a stainless steel bowl placed over ice and water. Stir continuously until the filling is cold. Refrigerate until ready to use. The filling can be made in advance.

TO ASSEMBLE:

～ Whip the filling (like whipping cream) until the mixture is smooth, creamy and firm, being careful not to overwhip.

～ Remove the cakes from the pans by loosening the edges with a knife. Peel off the waxed paper.

～ Place one layer on a serving plate. Combine the coffee and brandy. Brush the cake with the mixture (repeat for each cake). Spread the filling evenly on each layer and finish with the filling on the top and around the sides.

～ Refrigerate the cake for 4 hours before serving.

Serves 12

APPLE/CARAMEL CREPES

ALLA SALLY DOULIS

1	Basic Crepe recipe (page 54)	1	1 cup	whipping cream (35%)	250 mL
6	large apples, peeled, cored and thinly sliced	6	1½ tsp	granulated sugar	8 mL
			½ tsp	vanilla	2 mL
½ tsp	vanilla	2 mL		Pinch salt	
1 Tbsp	fresh lemon juice	15 mL		Caramel Sauce recipe (page 161)	

~ Preheat an oven to 350°F (180°C).

~ Cook the crepes according to the recipe and set aside.

~ Toss the apples with the vanilla and lemon juice. Set aside.

~ Whip the cream, sugar, vanilla and salt until soft peaks are formed. Keep chilled until ready to serve.

~ Place the crepes on 2 cookie sheets, then spread a thin layer of caramel sauce over each crepe. Arrange the apples over the caramel sauce in a circular pattern.

~ Place the crepes in the preheated oven and bake for 15 minutes or until the apples can be pierced with a fork. Remove the crepes from the oven and serve with swirls of caramel sauce and whipped cream on top.

Serves 6

BISCOTTI DI MAIS

CORN FLOUR COOKIES

These cookies have a subtle and unassuming taste. They go well with ice cream or a fruit compote.

16 oz	fine corn flour	500 g	1 cup	granulated sugar	250 mL
2 oz	white all-purpose flour, sifted	50 g	3	large eggs	3
	Pinch of salt			Juice of 2 lemons	
6 oz	unsalted butter	175 g		Zest of 2 lemons, grated	

- Preheat an oven to 350°F (160°C).

- Mix the flours together with the salt. Set aside.

- Cream the butter and sugar until smooth; add the eggs, lemon juice and zest and flour mixture.

- Drop by the teaspoonful (5 mL) 1 inch (2.5 cm) apart onto a greased cookie sheet. Flatten with a spatula dipped in water.

- Bake for 15 minutes or until lightly browned around the edges.

- Remove to a wire rack and cool.

Yield: 75 cookies (454g)

CREPES SUZETTES

1	Basic Crepe recipe (page 54)	1

TO THE BASIC CREPE RECIPE, ADD

2 Tbsp	flour	25 mL
¼ cup	liquor; brandy, rum or kirsch	50 mL
	Peel of 1 orange or lemon, grated	

FOR THE SAUCE

¼ cup	granulated sugar	50 mL
	Juice of 1 orange	
	Juice of 1 lemon	
½ cup	Grand Marnier liquer	125 mL

⌒ After the crepe batter is prepared, make the sauce.

⌒ In a skillet, melt the sugar over medium heat until just brown; immediately add the orange and lemon juice and half of the Grand Marnier. Add the crepes to the mixture, one at a time, mixing well, turning and folding first in half and then in quarters. Remove crepes as they are ready to a warm plate. Repeat with the remaining crepes, adding the additional Grand Marnier as needed. Serve.

Serves 5

TORTA DI CIOCCOLATA ALLE NOCCIOLE

CHOCOLATE HAZELNUT ORANGE TORTE

10	egg whites	10	**FOR THE FILLING**		
13	large egg yolks at room temperature	13	4 cups	whipping cream (35%)	1 L
¾ cup	granulated sugar	175 mL	11 oz	milk chocolate, cut in small pieces	300 g
9 oz	hazelnuts, finely ground	250 g	¼ cup plus ¼ cup	Grand Marnier liquer	50 mL plus 50 mL
			1	Zest of 1 orange, finely chopped	

~ Preheat an oven to 350°F (180°C).

~ Beat the egg whites until foamy. Slowly add the sugar and continue to beat until the whites are almost stiff. Set aside.

~ Beat the egg yolks until thick and lemon yellow; gently fold in the egg whites; add the hazelnuts and gently fold until just mixed.

~ Pour the mixture into four 9-inch (23 cm) cake pans, ungreased and lined with waxed paper.

~ Bake for 30 to 35 minutes or until done. Remove from the oven and let cool completely in the pans.

FOR THE FILLING

~ In a heavy pot, over high heat, bring the cream to a boil; stir in the chocolate until completely dissolved. Remove from the heat and place the mixture in a stainless steel bowl placed over ice and water. Stir continuously until the filling is cold. Add ¼ cup (50 mL) Grand Marnier and orange zest. Refrigerate until ready to use. The filling can be made in advance.

TO ASSEMBLE

∽ Whip the filling (like whipping cream) until the mixture is smooth, creamy and firm, being careful not to overwhip.

∽ Remove the cakes from the pans by loosening the edges with a knife. Peel off the waxed paper.

∽ Place one layer of cake on a serving plate and brush it with some of the Grand Marnier (repeat for each cake). Spread the filling evenly on each layer and finish with the filling on the top and around the sides.

∽ Refrigerate the cake for 4 hours before serving.

Serves 12

TORTA DELLA NONNA

NONNA ROSA'S CAKE

This is a treasured recipe from Luigi's mother, which has been kept in the family for years. Alessandra has reproduced it for your enjoyment. The cake is delicious for a simple dessert or for breakfast with lemon or lime yoghurt and strawberries. It also makes a good base for strawberry shortcake.

2 cups	white flour	500 mL	¾ cup	vegetable oil	175 mL
6 tsp	baking powder	25mL	¾ cup	juice of 1 lemon and warm	175 mL
	Rind of 1 lemon or orange, grated			water	
8	whole eggs, at room temperature, separated	8		or ¾ cup (175 mL) fresh orange juice	
1½ cups	granulated sugar	375 mL			

⌒ Preheat an oven to 375°F (190°C). Grease a 10-inch (4 L) tube pan.

⌒ Sift the flour with the baking powder. Add the lemon or orange rind. Set aside.

⌒ Beat the egg yolks and half the sugar together until they turn pale yellow and are thickened. Add the oil and the lemon/water or orange juice. Stir. Slowly add the flour mixture.

⌒ Beat the egg whites in a bowl until they are stiff but not dry. Gradually add the remaining ¾ cup (175 mL) sugar. Gently fold the whites into the egg and flour mixture, incorporating well.

⌒ Pour the batter into the prepared tube pan. Bake for 45 minutes, or until a tester comes out clean. Remove the cake from the oven and invert over a tall bottle so the cake will not collapse. When it is cool, remove the cake by loosening the sides from the pan, and from around the tube, it should slide out.

⌒ Sprinkle the cake with powdered sugar and serve.

Serves 10

MOUSSE DI RICOTTA CON SALSA DI LAMPONE

RICOTTA MOUSSE CAKE WITH RASPBERRY SAUCE

¼ cup	cold water	50 mL	¾ cup	granulated sugar	175 mL
¼ cup	white rum	50 mL	16 oz	fresh ricotta cheese	500 g
2	packages or 2 Tbsp (25 mL) unflavored gelatin	2	1	layer sponge cake, ¼-inch (.6 cm) thick, or one layer of lady	1
1¾ cups	whipping cream (35%)	400 mL		fingers (To cut a thicker sponge	
6	large eggs, separated	6		cake, freeze first, then slice)	

~ In a small pan, mix the water and rum; sprinkle the gelatin on top and let stand.

~ Whip the cream until firm; refrigerate.

~ Beat the egg whites until foamy. Slowly add the sugar and continue to beat until the whites are almost stiff. Set aside.

~ Beat the egg yolks until thick and lemon yellow; add ricotta and continue beating until well blended. Melt the gelatin mixture over medium heat. Stir. Remove from the heat and cool slightly. Slowly mix the gelatin into the ricotta mixture, then gently fold in the egg whites. Fold in the whipping cream and mix well.

~ Use only the sides of a 9-inch (2.5 L) springform pan, place it on a large serving plate and line it with waxed paper, making a collar 2 inches (5 cm) above the rim. Pour the ricotta/cream mixture into the pan. Refrigerate for a minimum of 6 hours. Before serving, loosen the sides of the pan and remove the form. Serve with Raspberry Sauce.

FOR THE RASPBERRY SAUCE			1	lemon	1
4 cups	fresh raspberries	1 L	3 Tbsp	granulated sugar	45 mL
¼ tsp	baking soda	1 mL			

~ To prevent the raspberries from fermenting, soak them first in cold water with ¼ tsp (1 mL) baking soda for a few minutes, then drain. Place the raspberries in a blender and add the lemon juice and the sugar. Blend well. Pass the mixture through a very fine sieve to remove the seeds and serve.

Serves 12

GIOIELLO DI SALLY

8	egg whites at room temperature	8	1 tsp	icing sugar	5 mL
¼ tsp	cream of tartar	1 mL	1 tsp	vanilla	5 mL
2 cups	granulated sugar	500 mL	¾ cup	hazelnuts or walnuts, toasted, and chopped	175 mL
1 tsp	vanilla	5 mL		Caramel Sauce (recipe follows)	
1 tsp	vinegar	5 mL			
3 cups	whipping cream (35%)	750 mL			

∾ Separate the eggs the night before and let the whites sit at room temperature overnight.

∾ Preheat an oven to 250°F (120°C).

∾ Beat the egg whites with the cream of tartar until they hold a stiff peak. Gradually, add sugar 1 Tbsp (15 mL) at a time and beat until the mixture is stiff and glossy. Add the vanilla and vinegar.

∾ Grease, then line the bottoms of two 8-inch (20 cm) cake tins with parchment paper.

∾ Divide the meringue equally between the cake tins and bake in the preheated oven for 55 minutes. Turn off the oven and let the meringues cool. Remove the meringues from the oven when completely cool. Invert the pans and remove the parchment paper from the bottom. Don't be concerned if the meringue breaks up in places; the cream will cover it.

∾ Whip the cream; add the icing sugar and vanilla when the cream is almost firm.

∾ Place one meringue on a serving plate and top with half the cream; swirl a layer of caramel on top of the cream and top with some of the chopped nuts. Repeat with the second meringue and the remaining cream. Finish with another swirl of caramel and chopped nuts. Refrigerate for at least 1 hour before serving.

Serves 8–10

CARAMEL SAUCE

I like to freeze the remaining caramel sauce in small containers for serving with ice cream topped with pecans.

| 1 cup | whipping cream (35%) | 250 mL | | Juice of ½ a lemon | |
| 2 cups | granulated sugar | 500 mL | ½ cup | unsalted butter | 125 mL |

⌒ Heat the cream to a simmer.

⌒ Place the sugar and lemon juice in a heavy saucepan and stir. Over high heat, caramelize the sugar, stirring until it is dissolved, cooking until it is just golden brown. Remove from the heat and slowly pour in the hot cream, stirring constantly. Heat to a boil, stirring constantly; remove from the heat.

⌒ Add the butter and stir until mixed. Pour the caramel sauce into a bowl.

⌒ When cool, the caramel sauce can be frozen.

Yield: 2 cups (500 mL)

TORTA DI CIOCCOLATA ALLE NOCI AMERICANI

CHOCOLATE PECAN TORTE

10	egg whites	10	FOR THE MOUSSE FILLING		
13	large egg yolks at room temperature	13	4 cups	whipping cream (35%)	1 L
¾ cup	granulated sugar	175 mL	11 oz	semisweet chocolate, cut in small pieces	300 g
9 oz	pecans, finely ground	250 g	3 Tbsp	granulated sugar	45 mL
			¼ cup	Frangelico (hazelnut liquor)	50 mL
			¼ cup	water	50 mL

⁓ Preheat an oven to 350°F (180°C).

⁓ Beat the egg whites until foamy. Slowly add the sugar and continue to beat until the whites are almost stiff. Set aside.

⁓ Beat the egg yolks until thick and lemon yellow; gently fold in the egg whites; add the pecans and gently fold until just mixed.

⁓ Pour the mixture into four 9-inch (23 cm) cake pans, ungreased and lined with waxed paper.

⁓ Bake for 30 to 35 minutes or until done. Remove from the oven and let cool completely in the pans.

⁓ In a heavy pot, over high heat, bring the cream to a boil; stir in the chocolate and sugar until completely dissolved. Remove from the heat and place the mixture in a stainless steel bowl set over ice and water. Stir continuously until the filling is cold. Refrigerate until ready to use. The filling can be made in advance.

TO ASSEMBLE

⁓ Whip the filling until it is smooth, creamy and firm. Do not overwhip.

⁓ Remove the cakes from the pans by loosening the edges with a knife. Peel off the waxed paper.

⁓ Combine the Frangelico and water.

⁓ Place one layer on a serving plate. Brush the cake with the Frangelico mixture (repeat for each cake). Spread the filling evenly on each layer and finish with the filling on the top and around the sides.

⁓ Refrigerate the cake for 4 hours before serving.

Serves 12

TIRAMISU

In Italy you will often find tiramisu made with cocoa instead of chocolate because chocolate is not readily available in small towns. When Alessandra began making it she used lady fingers, but found them to be too soft. She looked for a firm, plain and subtle biscuit and found Plasmon Biscotti, a children's biscuit. If you cannot find Plasmon Biscotti at specialty food shops, substitute a tea biscuit.

6	large eggs at room temperature, separated	6	1½ cups	whipping cream (35%)	350 mL
			12 oz	Plasmon (Biscotti) biscuits, or tea biscuits	375 g
¾ cup	granulated sugar	175 mL			
¼ cup	brandy	50 mL	6 oz	semisweet chocolate	175 g
16 oz	mascarpone cheese	500 g	½ cup	espresso coffee	125 mL

∾ Whip the cream and refrigerate.

∾ Beat the egg whites until foamy. Slowly add the sugar and continue to beat until the whites are almost stiff. Set aside.

∾ Beat the egg yolks until thick and lemon yellow. Add the mascarpone and brandy and mix. Fold in the egg whites and the whipped cream.

∾ Distribute half of the cookies over the bottom of a 4-quart (4 L) rectangular baking dish; brush with half the espresso; top with half the filling; top with half the chocolate, grated. Repeat with the remaining cookies, espresso and filling. Finish with the remaining chocolate, using a vegetable peeler or knife to make chocolate curls over the top.

Serves 12

TORTA DI PAN D'ANGELI ALLA CIOCCOLATA BIANCA

WHITE CHOCOLATE ANGEL CAKE

This recipe makes two 2-layer cakes or one 4-layer cake.

3	pints strawberries, cleaned and sliced	3	1 cup	all-purpose flour, sifted	250 mL
	Juice of 2 lemons				
3 Tbsp	granulated sugar	45 mL	FOR THE FILLING		
6	large eggs	6	4 cups	whipping cream (35%)	1 L
1 cup	granulated sugar	250 mL	11 oz	white chocolate	300 g

- Preheat an oven to 350°F (180°C).

- Mix the strawberries with the lemon and sugar and set aside.

- Beat the eggs with the sugar until thick and lemon yellow; fold in the flour a little at a time.

- Pour the mixture into four 9-inch (23 cm) cake pans, ungreased and lined with waxed paper.

- Bake for 25 to 30 minutes or until done. Remove from the oven and let cool completely in the pans.

- In a heavy pot, over high heat, bring the cream to a boil; add the white chocolate and sugar and stir until completely dissolved. Remove from the heat and place the mixture in a stainless steel bowl set over ice and water. Stir continuously until the filling is cold. Refrigerate until ready to use. The filling can be made in advance.

TO ASSEMBLE

- Whip the filling until it is smooth, creamy and firm. Do not overwhip.

- Drain the juice from the strawberries into a separate cup.

- Remove the cakes from the pans by loosening the edges with a knife. Peel off the waxed paper.

- Place one layer on a serving plate. Brush the cake with the strawberry juice (repeat for each cake). Spread the filling evenly on each layer and top with some of the strawberries. Repeat. Finish with the filling on the top and around the sides. Decorate with white chocolate curls.

- Refrigerate the cake for 4 hours before serving.

Serves 12

ZABAGLIONE

| 3 | egg yolks | 3 | ¼ cup | dry Marsala | 50 mL |
| 2 Tbsp | granulated sugar | 25 mL | 2 Tbsp | water | 25 mL |

~ Place all the ingredients in the top of a double boiler over simmering water. Whisk constantly until the mixture is foamy and forms soft peaks when dropped from the whisk and bubbles begin to appear (about 8 minutes).

~ Serve the zabaglione warm in glass bowls or over fresh berries.

Serves 4

THE TRUTH ABOUT ITALIAN WINES

I've cycled my way through the wine producing
areas of France's Burgundy and the Loire Valley as
well as California's Sonoma and Napa Valleys where
I've tried the Burgundys, the Meursaults and the
Chardonnays, and I love them. One can only find
the distinct flavors of a Barolo, or a Tignanello, of
the reds, or Pinot Grigio, or the earthy flavor of
Fiano di Avellino, of the whites, in Italian wines.
There is something different about the taste of the
Italian wines (the flavors are intense). It is interesting to note that neither the Americans, the Chileans
nor the Australians have yet successfully cloned any
of the great Italian wines. Could it be the soil?...the
climate? I don't know, but I am certainly spoiled. As
my husband is often heard to quote, "Is there a man
with a soul so dead, who never to his wife has said,
hold on, give me my half of that Italian red?" So, get
out of your head and come to your senses as you
experience these special wines of Italy.

My husband and I live aboard a sailboat in the Mediterranean for six months of the year. We tour a different country each year. In 1997 we were at the top of the Adriatic having wintered our boat in Slovenia near Trieste, Italy. As a result, we discovered the culture, the food and the wine of a special country. We sailed the Italian coast, from the eastern port of Trieste to the western port of San Remo on the Italian Riviera. This chapter will highlight the Italian coast and our discovery of the unique wines of the various regions.

Adriano Vicentini, maitre d' at La Fenice, provided the following technical information about the wines of Italy. Adriano has recommended wines to accompany the recipes in this book, some of which are listed on the wine list of the restaurant. I have provided some comments of my own about some of the wines.

For further reading and excellent detail on Italian wines, Victor Hazan's book, *Italian Wine*, (Alfred A. Knopf, Inc.) is outstanding. Victor Hazan is a masterful writer of wine who outlines the wines of Italy by their place of origin, type and characteristics of grapes and categories of taste. He is particularly masterful at putting into words the art of tasting. His taste descriptions are overwhelmingly sensuous. For example, in his description of the merits of a Barolo, he states,

"The impact in the mouth is large, but not ponderous. The drama of Barolo's power is that it manages its great girth with supple and buoyant grace. The flavors bloom in the palate, conveying even in very advanced age an opulent and delectable impression of fruit. The aftertaste fades with haunting slowness, releasing as it retreats a seemingly indelible last emanation of flavor." Keep this description in mind as you contemplate serving to your guests the Prime Rib with Barolo (page 119).

To determine recent vintages and ratings, refer to *Parker's Wine Buyers Guide*, 4th Ed., complete, easy to use reference on recent vintages, prices and ratings of over 7,500 wines (Fireside, Simon and Schuster) or Wine Spectator's *Ultimate Guide to Buying Wine*, 6th Ed., with ratings and prices for over 40,000 wines (Wine Spectator Press.)

PIEDMONT (PIEMONTE)

These wines are close to the character of French wines – crisp, acidic, aromatic, aristocratic and smooth with refined flavor. The reds should be chilled to 60–70°F and the whites to 40–50°F in order to derive their full flavor. These great wines of Italy have strict requirements, i.e., more aging in wood than others. They produce a powerful taste to accompany the local foods, such as roasts,

*Luigi's regional map
of Italy*

wild meats, mushrooms, truffles, risottos and ragus. The best known are the Barolo and the Barbaresco. Recently, the Barbera reds have become chic, especially the Barberas from choice plots around Asti and Alba. Of course, Asti Spumante is the world's most popular sweet sparkling wine. Among the whites, the Gavi is considered one of Italy's most coveted, with a crisp, lively style, that goes well with seafood.

Red Wines from Piedmont (Piemonte)
>   Barbaresco, "Asili", Produttori del Barbaresco
>   Barbaresco "Montestefano", Prunotto
>   Barbaresco, Pio Cesare
>   Barbera "Barriques", Fratelli Abbona
>   Barbera d'Alba, Luigi Einaudi
>   Barbera d'Asti, Michele Chiarlo
>   Barolo, Einaudi
>   Barolo, "Sperss" Angelo Gaja
>   Barolo Riserva, Marchesi Di Barolo
>   Barolo, Cerequio, Chiarlo
>   Barolo Granbussia, A. Conterno
>   Dolcetto di Dogliani, Bricco San Bernardo
>   Abbona
>   Grignolino del Piemonte, Vino Da Tavola,
>   Scanavino

White Wines from Piedmont (Piemonte)
>   Chardonnay Elioro, Cordero Di
>   Montezemolo, Monfalletto
>   Gavi Fornaci del Tassarolo, Chiarlo
>   Gavi "La Raia" Martinengo
>   Roero Arneis, Carlo Deltetto
>   Rossj-Bass, Gaja

Red Frizzante Wines from Piedmont (Piemonte)
>   Goj, Cascinacastlet, Barbera del Monferrato,
>   Maria Borio Costigliore D'Asti, Nella
>   Cantina Di Calamandrana

White Frizzante Wines from Piedmont (Piemonte)
Asti Spumante

LOMBARDY (LOMBARDIA)

Although Lombardy, a region of hills, mountains and lakeside plains, is one of the largest and most populous regions of Italy, it is relatively unknown by North Americans. The significant wine growing areas in the region are Franciacorta, Oltrepo, Lugana, and Valtellina.

Franciacorta is situated on the edge of Lake Iseo, about fifty miles northeast of Milan. Franciacorta is well known for its dry sparkling wines, which have achieved an international reputation for excellence. Ca' del Bosco is a major, acclaimed producer in the region, of fine sparkling wines as well as complex, profoundly flavored still wines.

The Ca' del Bosco "Franciacorta Brut" (sparkling wine) is made from carefully selected Chardonnay, Pinot Blanc and Pinot Noir grapes and yields a fresh, fragrant wine with a delicious taste. These sparkling wines can be enjoyed as aperitifs, as well as with a meal. The Ca' del Bosco Chardonnay has a deep golden yellow color and a complex fragrance with elements of ripe fruit, vanilla and toast. In the mouth, it has a rich structure, finesse and great smoothness. It goes well with all fish dishes as well as many light meat dishes.

The Ca' del Bosco Cabernet, "Maurizio Zanella", named after the charismatic and flamboyant principal of the company, is made from a mix of Cabernet Sauvignon, Cabernet Franc and Merlot grapes. It is an elegant and refined wine with a deep complex varietal fragrance, full, smooth flavor and a lingering aromatic persistence. It is the Ca' del Bosco wine that has received the most recognition both from the international professional press and from fine restaurants.

Sparkling White Wines from Lombardy (Lombardia)
Franciacorta Brut, Ca' del Bosco
Vintage Franciacorta Brut, Ca' del Bosco

White Wines from Lombardy (Lombardia)
Bianco Franciacorta, Ca' del Bosco
Chardonnay, Ca' del Bosco
Terre di Franciacorta, Ca' del Bosco

Red Wines from Lombardy (Lombardia)
Cabernet Terre di Franciacorta
Maurizio Zanella, Ca' del Bosco
Rosso Franciacorta, Ca' del Bosco

FRIULI – VENEZIA GIULIA AND TRENTINO-ALTO ADIGE

The Friuli area is a hilly region on the Austrian/ Slovenian/ Italian border and it was the first region we discovered after spending several weeks in Trieste. In fact, when we were sailing the Croatian coast in the summer of 1996, we met the owner and operator of a Friuli vineyard, Patrizia Stekar of Castello di Spessa, Cormons, Italy. We had sailed to a long narrow island in the Kornati Island group called Otok Piskera, where there was a first class marina and nothing else except the beauty of an unspoiled island in the middle of nowhere. And we were lucky because gale force winds and a rain storm passed through that night. These islands are north of Split and we were beginning to encounter primarily Italian cruisers. In the morning, the Italians across the way introduced themselves and requested a tour of our boat. It's a Hans Christian sailboat, ketch, made in Taiwan, and therefore different from the average boat. After the tour the couple and their guests invited us to their power yacht for coffee, and we exchanged information about ourselves. My husband gave their guest, who was a senior Italian tax inspector, his book *Take Your Money and Run* (from extortionist high taxes) and they, in return, gave us a couple of bottles of their wine, La Boatina, Collio, 1993, a Cabernet Franc. It was delicious, though Friuli is known more for its excellent white wines.

Today, the best Italian white wines come from the Friuli and Trentino-Alto Adige regions. In the Friuli there is a variety of grapes with a crisp acidity combined with body, concentration and ripeness. The white wines of Italy are less "oaky" than in other countries because they are rarely aged in oak barrels and they are more acidic. It is easier to match foods with these whites. They are also more thirst-quenching. The white wine from the Trentino-Alto Adige region, which borders Austria, is known for its fruity flavors, which are aromatic and effervescent, and found in medium bodied and dessert wines. There is a great variety of wines here but the whites are better than the reds. The flavor of the white wines of Trentino stands on its own. These wines go well with spicy foods without disappearing in the mouth. They

complement food perfectly, particularly Chinese, Thai and Indian foods. Some selections to serve with spicy food are the Tocai, Pinot Gris or a Gewurztraminer.

Red Wines from the Friuli-Venezia Giulia and Trentino-Alto Adige

Cabernet Franc, Aquileia, Ca'Bolani

Merlot "Collio" Venica & Venica

La Boatina, "Collio", Cab Franc, Cormons

La Boatina, "Collio", Pinot Nero, Cormons

Trentino, Marzemino

Schioppettino, G. Dorigo

Teroldego Rotaliano, Mezzacorona

White Wines from the Friuli-Venezia Giulia and Trentino-Alto Adige

Chardonnay, Tiefenbrunner (Trentino-Alto Adige)

Chardonnay, Valdadige, Armani

Gewurztraminer, Alois Lageder

Lunelli, Villa Margon, Fratelli Lunelli

Pinot Bianco, G. Dorigo

Pinot Grigio, Armani

Pinot Grigio, "Collio", Borgoconventi

Pinot Grigio, Collio, Cantina Produttori, Cormons

Pinot Grigio, La Cros, Valdadige, Boscaini

Pinot Grigio, Rulander, Valdadige, S. Margherita

Pinot Grigio, Alois Lageder

Ribolla Gialla, G. Dorigo

Sauvignon, Collio, Dorigo

Sauvignon Ronco di Mele, Venica & Venica

Tocai Friulano, G. Dorigo

Tocai Friulano, Le Vigne di Zamo, Colli
Orientali del Friuli, Rosazzo Manzano

Vintage Tunina, Jermann

VENETO

In the Veneto, the most popular and well known red is the Amarone – a full-bodied wine. Its bitterness is disguised by the powerful concentration of the overripeness of the grapes and the addition of more sugar than usual in its preparation. The method of producing the Amarone results in its delicious taste and higher alcohol content. The grapes are specifically selected, then the "ears" are snipped off, inspected, spread out on a pallet to dry in the sun and checked every day to insure that there is no formation of mold that will infect the bunch. This process culminates in a 50% lower yield than if the grapes had been crushed when they were fresh. It is a traditional method and, historically, Amarone was drunk by the philosophers during their meditation. It is a powerful wine, great tasting on its own or with strong

cheese, strong pasta sauces and ragus.

Of the whites, the Soave is a dry, crisp, nutty-flavored wine, which is a good match for seafood or fish.

While we were in Trieste we were introduced to the frizzantes of the Veneto by a sailor, Bob Plan, whom we met at the Societa Triestina della Vela Yacht Club. While there is a wide range of frizzantes, the ones we tried, either white or red, were more dry than sweet. They are called amiables or demi sec. They are typically consumed as an aperitif or with ragus. They are quite interesting for a change and are inexpensive and light, having 8.5% alcohol content. We especially enjoyed them for lunch.

Frizzante Wines from the Veneto

Tenutas Anna, Cabernet, Vino Spumante di
qualita; a demi sec frizzante.

Prosecco di Valdobbiadene, Cantina
Produttori; a white frizzante

Red Wines from the Veneto

Amarone, Tommasi

Amarone, Bertani

Amarone, Allegrini

Amarone "Barriques", Zeni

Amarone "Il Bosco", Cesari

Amarone, Luigi Righetti

Amarone della Valpolicella, Montresor

Amarone, Classico, Remo Farina

Cabernet Breganze "Fratta", Maculan
Ferrata, Cabernet Sauvignon, Maculan
Valpolicella Classico Boscaini

White Wines from the Veneto
Ferrata Chardonnay, Maculan
Inama Soave Classico Superiore, Vigneti di
  Foscarino
Masi Bianco, Serego Alighieri
Soave, Bolla
Vespaiolo, Maculan

EMILIA-ROMAGNA

The main attraction in the Emilia-Romagna region is Ravenna, a city that contains churches with some of the best mosaics in the world, including the Basilica of San Vitale.

Bologna, the gourmet capital of Italy, was one hour away from Ravenna by train. The main attraction was lunch. We arrived just in time, about noon. That gave us just enough time to walk the streets of the city, see some of the beautiful buildings and arrive at the restaurant by 1:00. Luigi, an Italian-Canadian we met in Ravenna, chose the restaurant. There was a fresh pasta shop alongside where we could watch the preparation of fresh raviolis, agnolottis and other assorted pastas. I knew what I was having for lunch – ravioli with Bolognese sauce (when in Rome...). Of course, Luigi suggested a Lambrusco, a red frizzante, the most popular wine in the region. The meal was memorable and I long to return to Bologna.

Emilia-Romagna is probably best known for its Lambrusco. However, the Sangiovese di Romagna (red) and the Albana (white) are the more refined tastes of the region.

Red Wines from Emilia-Romagna
Barbarossa Fattoria Paradiso, Mario Pezzi
Barbera dei Colli Bolognesi di Monte San Pietro
Cabernet Sauvignon Terre Rosse
Sangiovese di Romagna, Spalletti

White Wines from Emilia-Romagna
Albana, Mario Pezzi

Frizzante Wines from Emilia-Romagna
Red: Lambrusco, Grasparossa Di Castelvetro,
  Manicardi

THE MARCHE (LE MARCHE)

The Marche is on the east coast of Italy, a varied region, with the industrial town of Ancona along with the seaside resorts of Pesaro, Conero Riviera and San Benedetto del Tronto. We headed for a yacht club in San Benedetto that had been recommended to us. San Benedetto was a pleasant surprise with its three miles of beach and five thousand palm trees; the Riviera of the east coast. We arrived on a Sunday and, in true Italian style, the local families were out for the afternoon passeggio (stroll), providing a colorful and joyous sight.

The next day we took a side tour by train to the medieval town of Ascoli Piceno, a picturesque spot rich in churches, palaces and narrow, marbled streets, with a good, full-bodied red wine – Ascoli Piceno, Rosso Piceno, Superiore.

White Wines from the Marche (Le Marche)
The Verdicchio from the Marche is a very well known, reasonably priced white wine that goes well with fish. The Verdicchio is a crisp and light wine, not too acidic, well rounded and balanced.
    Falerio dei Colli Ascolani, Saladini Pilastri
    Verdicchio, Castelli di Jesi, Vinemar
    Verdicchio, Cuprese
    Verdicchio, Marchetti

Red Wines from the Marche (Le Marche)
    Ascoli Piceno, Rosso Piceno, Superiore, Tenuta
        Cocci Grifoni.
    Rosso Piceno, Saladini Pilastri

ABRUZZI (ABRUZZO)/ MOLISE

The wine produced in Abruzzi carries a refreshing simplicity. There are only two wines of distinction in this region – the Montepulciano and Trebbiano vines.

The Molise region is often listed as an appendix to the Abruzzi, since it's a fairly small area. There are two red wines of note, the Biferno and Pentro.

Red wines from Abruzzi (Abruzzo)/Molise
    Biferno, Masseria Di Majo Norante
    Montepulciano d'Abruzzo, Terre D'Aligi
        Spinelli
    Pentro di Isernia

White wines from Abruzzi (Abruzzo)/Molise
    Trebbiano d'Abruzzo

APULIA (PUGLIA)

This is the home of good, powerful, inexpensive red wines which go well with heavy tomato sauces, eggplant and spicy sausages.

We spent five days in the old town of Vieste, at the most easterly point of the Gargano peninsula, which juts out into the Adriatic. We arrived around dusk after a longish sail from Termoli. A young Italian man came down the pier to take our lines and we were secured for the night. The next day we learned that there were two marinas, the other one operated by a Canadian woman and her Italian husband. She was most helpful in guiding us to good food and drink. The town of Vieste was very pleasant and the locals were friendly. The most memorable drink was the Lemoncello, a lemon liquor. It is best served ice cold. I highly recommend it for a nightcap.

Another enjoyable stop in the Puglia region was the coastal town of Trani, a large cosmopolitan city, unspoiled by tourists, which has an old medieval port (safe mooring for our boat especially when the winds picked up to 40 knots). From here we sailed to Brindisi where we were introduced to a relatively unknown (in North America) wine by a local wine merchant, the Patriglione. It was quite delicious.

Red Wines from Apulia (Puglia)
   Patriglione, Brindisi, Azienda Agricola Cosimo
      Taurino
   Primitivo Del Tarantino "Le Petrose", Vinicola
      Savese
   Salice Salentino

BASILICATA

Basilicata is one of the southern wine growing zones and is sparsely populated, poor and mountainous with harsh conditions which are, nonetheless, good for growing grapes. There is only one D.O.C. (Denominazione di Origine Controllata), in the area – the Aglianico del Vulture and the Riserva, produced by D'Angelo Paternoster. Aglianico is the name of the grape, in the region of Vulture, or Volcano. The vines grow in volcanic soil in the shadow of, and on, the hillside of the volcano known as Mount Vulture.

These wines, when well made, are well rounded with fruit and good acidic backbone. They can be quite rich, black in flavor and complex with tastes of cherry and violets, chocolate, coffee and tar. The Aglianico Riserva is aged for five years, which is the same aging requirement for the Brunello di Montalcino Riserva and Barolo Riserva.

Red Wines from Basilicata
   Aglianico del Vulture, D'Angelo
   Aglianico del Vulture "Riserva Vigna Caselle",
      D'Angelo

CALABRIA

We experienced a great deal of the Calabria region as we sailed from the east to the west coast, stopping at Crotone and Roccella Ionica on the east coast, through the Straights of Messina and up the west coast, to Reggio di Calabria, Bagnara Calabria (a small port primarily for the atypical and strange-looking swordfishing boats), and Vibo Valentia Marina. Calabria tends generally to be less admired than other parts of Italy, but we thoroughly enjoyed this region. The food was rich, sometimes spicy and very tasty. The area had fewer tourists than elsewhere and was unspoiled. The coastline from the Straights of Messina going north was spectacular.

Red Wines from Calabria
  Ciro
  Gravello, Rosso di Calabria, Casa Vinicola
    Librandi

SICILY (SICILIA)

To lead into the Sicilian wine, I must digress to another place where we drank an unforgettable bottle. We spent a couple of days moored at the public pier at Sesti Levante, a pleasant, popular resort town east of Genoa and just north of the Cinqueterre region. Palm trees with red and pink cacti growing under the umbrella of the palms lined the passaggio, the wide walkway along the beach. This area is well known for its hiking trails. We left Sesti Levante and headed northeast towards Portofino on the Italian Riviera. Portofino is the well known, picturesque, tiny resort by the seaside, with chic restaurants and shops, and expensive mega-yachts moored in the harbor.

The winds were blowing from the east, an undesirable direction for this area for those of us at sea because it created a considerable and uncomfortable swell. We sailed into the harbor of Portofino only to discover that although there was an empty spot at the public pier, there was no room to safely manoeuvre the boat. We headed up the coast to two marinas in the area but there was no space for visitors. We anchored in the bay at St. Marguerita Ligure with little protection from the east wind, but it was the best we could find.

We had planned to eat ashore that evening so there were no fresh provisions aboard. I decided to cook a pasta with a puttanesca sauce (a spicy dish). I looked in my store of wines for a strong red to accompany the strong sauce and I found a bottle of Rosso Del Conte, 1988, a Sicilian wine we bought a year ago when we were in Sicily. I thought it would go well with the dinner as I had found the Sicilian reds to be largely rich and full-bodied. I was not disappointed. It was a pleasant surprise to find such a delicious, strong flavor to accompany the puttanesca sauce.

Sicily is the largest Mediterranean island and has more vineyards than many other regions. Wine production is sizable, however the percentage of notable wines is small. The famous Marsala is Sicily's most popular wine.

Red Wines from Sicily (Sicilia)
   Cabernet Sauvignon, Principe di Corleone
   Centare, Rosso, Duca di Castel Monte
   Col. di Sasso, Cabernet Sauvignon and
      Sangiovese
   Duca Enrico, Duca di Salaparuta
   Etna Rosso
   Faro
   Faustus Rosso
   Il Rosso, Principe di Corleone
   Rosso del Conte
   Tancredi, Donna Fugata
   Tasca D'Almerita, Cabernet Sauvignon
   Terre D'Agala, Duca di Salaparuta

White Wines from Sicily (Sicilia)
   Bianco d'Alcamo
   Marsala
   Pinot Bianco, Corleone
   Regaleali Nozze d'Oro
   Zurrica, Abbazia Santa Anastasia

SARDINIA (SARDEGNA)

When we first landed on the island of Sardinia in 1991 (from the Spanish Balearic Island of Menorca, Mahon harbor) it was at the southern port of Cagliari. We had navigated the trip from Mahon to Alghero, a small fishing port in the northwest of the Sardinian Island, but we heard on the "Net" (shortwave talk show for sailors) that the fishermen had barricaded the harbor. We had encountered engine trouble enroute, so we ended up spending three weeks on the Cagliari public pier and grew to know and enjoy this rather large city. What I remember most is that there were very good restaurants and fresh markets, but most of all, Cagliari was one of the most inexpensive cities from which to purchase fine Italian products, including clothing and leather goods. The only other city we visited in all of Italy that had similar, reasonable (not tourist) prices, was Genoa. From Cagliari we rented a car and toured the southern third of the island, which is filled with history and the remains of various civilizations. The surprise was seeing Sardinia's Nuraghic civilization, a fascinating stone-built construction.

We returned to Sardinia in 1997 to sail the Costa Smeralda, the northeastern part of the island and Sardinia's best known resort area. It offers the best cruising because of the beauty of the northern tip of the island. We headed to Porto Cervo, the yachting center for the rich and famous, built by the Consorzio Costa Smeralda, whose president is the Aga Khan. It is a masterpiece of architectural planning, tastefully done and environmentally conscious, blending all the building materials with the landscape and thus preserving its beauty. This complex reminded me of Scotsdale, Arizona. It is truly a stunning looking place, together with a complex of elegant shops and the super-rich showing off their new floating toys. It is a must see, and we were able to do so by anchoring off in the bay, so thoughtfully provided by the Consorzio. We did have a moment of fun when we inquired about the price for one night's stay at the pier amongst the mega-yachts, "Yes madam, $175," but there was no space available! We heard from one of the mega-yacht captains that he had booked one year in advance!

Sardinia's history has been influenced by the Spaniards as much as by the Italians. The vines of Sardinia also have a Spanish accent. The major vineyard area is the Campidano, northwest of Cagliari, the capital and major port. Several varieties of wine are almost unique in Italy, such as Cannonau, Giro, Monica, Nuragus, Torbato and Vernaccia di Oristano. The northwestern coastal area near Sassari and Alghero is noted for quality white wines, such as Vermentino. From the Sorso and Sennori regions, Moscato is notable. The two most important reds are the Cannonau and Monica, both of Spanish origin. In 2000, II Sommelier Italiano voted the Turriga 95 the best red wine. Sardinia is best known for its aperitif and sweet wines, such as the sherry-like Vernaccia, and the Cannonau di Sardegna, a delicious full-bodied, inexpensive red, a favorite of the locals. The Sella & Mosca Rosé wine is excellent and one of the best in Italy.

Red Wines from Sardinia (Sardegna)
 Campidano di Terralba
 Cannonau Di Sardegna, Riserva, Sella & Mosca
 Giro
 Marchese Di Villamarina, Sella & Mosca
 Monica
 Tanca Farra, Sella & Mosca
 Turriga, '95, Argiolas, Cagliari

White Wines from Sardinia (Sardegna)
 Moscato
 Nuragus di Cagliari
 Vermentino Sella & Mosca
 Vernaccia di Oristano

Rosé Wines from Sardinia (Sardegna)
 Rosé Alghero, Sella & Mosca

Campania was considered by the ancient Romans to be the ultimate wine region, especially the vineyards along the coast north of Naples where Falernum, the most treasured wine of the Roman empire, was cultivated. Also considered notable were the vines of Vesuvius and the hills of Avellino. The Greeks also were impressed with this region and introduced the Aglianico and Greco vines. The most prominent wines today from Campania are the red Taurasi, which has a particular flavor and character of its own, and the white Fiano di Avellino and Greco di Tufo. They are produced by one of the best vintners, Mastroberardino. The Fiano has a distinct aromatic smell, like flint, like ancient earth; and the Greco di Tufo is a crisp, fruity wine with a tinge of almond in the bouquet.

Red Wines from Campania
 Aglianico del Taburno
 Falerno del Massere, Molo Vinicola
 Falerno, Villa Matilde
 Taurasi 'Radici', Mastroberardino

White Wines from Campania
 Falerno del Massico, Villa Matilde
 Fiano di Avellino, Mastroberardino
 Greco di Tufo, Mastroberardino

Luigi Orgera's hometown, *Spigno Saturnia*, is in the Lazio region which is bordered by Tuscany on the north and Campania on the south. Lazio is best known for its stretch of ancient places along the coast from Rome to Naples. In the summer of 1999 we were fortunate to secure a space to winter our boat at Base Nautica Flavio Gioia Marina in Gaeta, where the Gulf of Gaeta forms the southernmost stretch of coastline in the region of Lazio.

While Gaeta's origins are said to date back to ancient times, it is the Roman Age that has left its mark on the region. Due to the extraordinary beauty of the promontory of Gaeta and its coasts, mild climate and healthy air, Gaeta became a renowned resort for emperors and early wealthy Romans. The territory was enriched with villas and mausoleums which can still be enjoyed today. It is steeped in history, with sites such as the mausoleum built by Lucius Munatius Planco during Augustus' reign (20 BC), at the top of the Monte Orlando promontory, opening exceptional views over medieval Gaeta and the gulf. And just north of Gaeta lies the Grotto of Tiberius. This site includes the ruins of the imperial villa and a national archaeological museum that houses marble decorations from Emperor Tiberius' Grotto. Sperlonga, a charming seaside village, sits atop a promontory overlooking the beaches opposite the Grotto of Tiberius. Sperlonga's attraction is its medieval town and roughly six miles of beaches at the shores of the Tyrrhenian sea.

Medieval Gaeta is a picturesque town of small streets and narrow alleys, staircases, underpasses and overbridges, a large castle, Norman belltowers, ancient walls and plenty of churches. Modern Gaeta, known as "The Borgo" or "Spiaggia", is Gaeta's second city center. It was created by local fishermen and farmers and extends along the charming Via Indipendenza, a narrow, stone paved walking lane lined with specialty shops (one of a kind; a shopper's dream).

This entire area is just enough off the beaten path to make it a wonderful place to visit where there are fewer tourists. This region near Rome today produces whites which are pleasantly fleshy and fruity and accompany a wide range of foods. They are meant to be drunk off the shelf. There is a large volume of these wines, such as the Frascati, for example, sold to the commercial market worldwide. The ancient Romans preferred the red Falernum, however, which is a notable wine of the region even today.

Red Wines from Latium (Lazio)
   Cecubo
   Cervetri
   Cesanese
   Colle Picchioni
   Cori
   Fiorano Rosso
   Torre Ercolana
   Velletri

White Wines from Latium (Lazio)
   Est!Est!!Est!!! di Montefiascone
   Frascati, Gotto D'Oro

UMBRIA

Orvieto, one of Italy's best selling whites, has historical prominence acclaimed by popes, princes and painters. Today Orvieto, once a soft, golden, tasting wine, has been modified into a pale, pure, crisp taste, and recently Orvieto's Aboccato has become popular as a dessert wine. But the most prominent is the red, Torgiano Rosso Riserva. Other reds from the region are also good.

The white Sauvignon should be served with antipasti, fish and foods with light sauces.

Red Wines from Umbria
   Cabernet Sauvignon
   Rubesco Riserva, Lungarotti
   San Giorgio, Lungarotti
   Torgiano Rosso Riserva

White Wines from Umbria

    Cervaro della Sala, Antinori

    Chardonnay, Lungarotti

    Orvieto, Farina

    Sauvignon, Castello della Sala, Antinori

TUSCANY (TOSCANA)

Tuscany is red wine country but there is one white that is worth mentioning, Vernaccia di San Gimignano, a strong, pale gold, aromatic, flavorful white (a favorite of Michelangelo's). It can be served with white meats in light sauces. It also would be a good accompaniment to the Puree of Squash Soup (page 38).

In Tuscany, there is a great variety and range of medium to full-bodied, powerful reds. Tignanello, produced by Antinori, a major wine producer in Chianti, and sometimes referred to as a supertuscan, is made outside the regulations of the controlled appellation requirements, with primarily sangiovese grapes and up to 15% Cabernet Sauvignon. The sangiovese grape produces a less sharp taste than Chianti, and the grapes are hand selected. Tignanello is an invention of Antinori. It is an elegant, extraordinary red wine. There are other supertuscan wines produced, (see below, under reds) but Tignanello is an exclusive name.

Sassicaia is probably the most popular of the supertuscans, similar to the Bordeaux wines.

The most well known and popular red wines of Tuscany, however, are the Chiantis, which are a blend, and the quality varies dramatically. The better Chiantis are the Riservas, which go well with a variety of foods such as pastas, meats and beans.

White Wines from Tuscany (Toscana)

    Galestro, Antinori

    Vernaccia di San Gimignano, Castelgreve di Pesa

    Vin Santo, dessert or aperitif wine

Red Wines from Tuscany (Toscana)

There have been some great vintages to complement the wines in the last ten years. The red wines from Tuscany are often classified into categories of Bolgheri, Chianti, Montalcino, supertuscans and Vini Da Tavola.

BOLGHERI

Guado Al Tasso "Tenuta Belvedere", Piero
    Antinori

Ornellaia, Marchesi Lodovico Antinori

Sassicaia, Marchesi Incisa della Rocchetta

CHIANTI

Chianti Classico Riserva, Castello di
    Verrazzano

Chianti Classico Riserva "Petri", Tenute

Vicchiomaggio
Chianti Classico Riserva "Il Picchio", Castello
  Di Querceto
Chianti Classico, Badia a Passignano, Riserva
  Antinori
Chianti Classico Riserva "Vigna Del Sorbo",
  Fontodi
Castello Nipozzano, Frescobaldi

MONTALCINO
Brunello di Montalcino "Poggio Al Vento",
  Col d'Orcia
Brunello di Montalcino, Pertimali
Brunello di Montalcino, Talenti

SUPERTUSCANS AND VINI DA TAVOLA
Brancaia, Castello di Fonterutoli
Cabernet Sauvignon, "Le Stanze" Poliziano
Luce, Frescobaldi
Morellino di Scansano, Agricola Mantellassi
Mormoreto, Frescobaldi
Olmaia, Col D'Orcia
Querciolaia Alicante, Agricola Mantellassi
Ripa delle Mandorle, Tenuta Vicchiomaggio
Tignanello, Piero Antinori
Vigorello, San Felice
Vino Nobile di Montepulciano "La Villa",
  Tenuta Trerose

Rosé Wines from Tuscany (Toscana)
  Rosato di Bolgheri, Antinori

LIGURIA

The celebrated Cinqueterre wine of the Ligurian coast, a delicious white, must be sampled while visiting the area because it is produced in such small quantities that it rarely leaves Italy. The Cinqueterre has a crisp and fruity flavor, excellent as a summer refresher. There are three main producers and all are good. One specific producer is listed below. Also of note is the sweet and rare Sciacchetra, sometimes preferred by connoisseurs.

White Wines from Liguria
  Cinqueterre, Groppo Di Riomaggiore,
    Agricoltura Di Riomaggiore Manarola
  Linero Bianco, Vermentino, Tognoni
  Sciacchetra (sweet)

Red Wines from Liguria
  Rossese di Dolceacqua, Croesi

Here is a list of wines for your convenience while shopping. I often take this list with me to the local wine store to help me in my search. In this way, I have become more familiar with the wines from the various areas. Not all of the producers or wines listed here are available all the time, but when I am successful in finding them I am thrilled. You will usually be able to find most of the wines listed, even if you cannot find wines from every producer named.

RED WINES

Red Wines from Piedmont (Piemonte)

Barbaresco, "Asili", Produttori del Barbaresco
Barbaresco "Montestefano", Prunotto
Barbaresco, Pio Cesare
Barbera "Barriques", Fratelli Abbona
Barbera d'Alba, Luigi Einaudi
Barbera d'Asti, Michele Chiarlo
Barolo, Einaudi
Barolo, "Sperss" Angelo Gaja
Barolo Riserva, Marchesi Di Barolo
Barolo, Cerequio, Chiarlo
Barolo Granbussia, A. Conterno
Dolcetto di Dogliani, Bricco San Bernardo Abbona
Grignolino del Piemonte, Vino Da Tavola, Scanavino

Red Wines from Lombardy (Lombardia)

Cabernet Terre di Franciacorta Maurizio Zanella, Ca' del Bosco
Rosso Franciacorta, Ca' del Bosco

Red Wines from the Friuli-Venezia Giulia and Trentino-Alto Adige

Cabernet Franc, Aquileia, Ca'Bolani
Merlot "Collio" Venica & Venica
La Boatina, "Collio", Cab Franc, Cormons
La Boatina, "Collio", Pinot Nero, Cormons
Trentino, Marzemino
Schioppettino, G. Dorigo
Teroldego Rotaliano, Mezzacorona

Red Wines from the Veneto

Amarone, Tommasi
Amarone, Bertani
Amarone, Allegrini
Amarone "Barriques", Zeni
Amarone "Il Bosco", Cesari
Amarone, Luigi Righetti
Amarone della Valpolicella, Montresor
Amarone, Classico, Remo Farina
Cabernet Breganze "Fratta", Maculan
Ferrata, Cabernet Sauvignon, Maculan
Valpolicella Classico Boscaini

Red Wines from Emilia-Romagna

Barbarossa Fattoria Paradiso, Mario Pezzi
Barbera dei Colli Bolognesi di Monte San Pietro
Cabernet Sauvignon Terre Rosse
Sangiovese di Romagna, Spalletti

Red Wines from the Marche (Le Marche)

Ascoli Piceno, Rosso Piceno, Superiore, Tenuta Cocci Grifoni.
Rosso Piceno, Saladini Pilastri

Red wines from Abruzzi (Abruzzo)/Molise

Biferno, Masseria Di Majo Norante
Spinelli Montepulciano d'Abruzzo, Terre D'Aligi
Pentro di Isernia

Red Wines from Apulia (Puglia)

Patriglione, Brindisi, Azienda Agricola Cosimo Taurino
Primitivo Del Tarantino "Le Petrose", Vinicola Savese
Salice Salentino

Red Wines from Basilicata

Aglianico del Vulture, D'Angelo
Aglianico del Vulture 'Riserva Vigna Caselle', D'Angelo

Red Wines from Calabria

Ciro
Gravello, Rosso di Calabria, Casa Vinicola Librandi

Red Wines from Sicily (Sicilia)

Cabernet Sauvignon, Principe di Corleone
Centare, Rosso, Duca di Castel Monte
Col. di Sasso, Cabernet Sauvignon and Sangiovese
Duca Enrico, Duca di Salaparuta
Etna Rosso
Faro
Faustus Rosso
Il Rosso, Principe di Corleone

Rosso del Conte
Tancredi, Donna Fugata
Tasca D'Almerita, Cabernet
    Sauvignon
Terre D' Agala, Dula di Salaparuta

Red Wines from Sardinia (Sardegna)

Campidano di Terralba
Cannonau Di Sardegna, Riserva,
    Sella & Mosca
Giro
Marchese Di Villamarina, Sella &
    Mosca
Monica
Tanca Farra, Sella & Mosca
Turriga, 95, Argiolas, Cagliari

Red Wines from Campania

Aglianico del Taburno
Falerno del Massere, Molo Vinicola
Falerno, Villa Matilde
Taurasi "Radici", Mastroberardino

Red Wines from Latium (Lazio)

Cecubo
Cervetri
Cesanese
Colle Picchioni
Cori
Fiorano Rosso
Torre Ercolana
Velletri

Red Wines from Umbria

Cabernet Sauvignon
Rubesco Riserva, Lungarotti
San Giorgio, Lungarotti
Torgiano Rosso Riserva

Red Wines from Tuscany (Toscana)

Bolgheri
Guado Al Tasso "Tenuta Belvedere",
    Piero Antinori
Ornellaia, Marchesi Lodovico
    Antinori
Sassicaia, Marchesi Incisa della
    Rocchetta

Chianti

Chianti Classico Riserva, Castello
    di Verrazzano
Chianti Classico Riserva "Petri",
    Tenute Vicchiomaggio
Chianti Classico Riserva "Il
    Picchio", Castello Di Querceto
Chianti Classico, Badia a
    Passignano, Riserva Antinori
Chianti Classico Riserva "Vigna Del
    Sorbo", Fontodi
Castello Nipozzano, Frescobaldi

Montalcino

Brunello di Montalcino "Poggio Al
    Vento", Col d'Orcia
Brunello di Montalcino, Pertimali
Brunello di Montalcino, Talenti

Supertuscans and Vini Da Tavola

Brancaia, Castello di Fonterutoli
Cabernet Sauvignon, "Le Stanze"
    Poliziano
Luce, Frescobaldi
Morellino di Scansano, Agricola
    Mantellassi
Mormoreto, Frescobaldi
Olmaia, Col D'Orcia
Querciolaia Alicante, Agricola
    Mantellassi
Ripa Delle Mandorle, Tenuta
    Vicchiomaggio
Tignanello, Piero Antinori
Vigorello, San Felice
Vino Nobile di Montepulciano "La
    Villa", Tenuta Trerose

Red Wines from Liguria

Rossese di Dolceacqua, Croesi

WHITE WINES

White Wines from Piedmont (Piemonte)

Chardonnay Elioro, Cordero Di
  Montezemolo, Monfalletto
Gavi Fornaci del Tassarolo, Chiarlo
Gavi "La Raja" Martinengo
Roero Arneis, Carlo Deltetto
Rossj-Bass, Gaja

White Wines from Lombardy (Lombardia)

Bianco Franciacorta, Ca' del Bosco
Chardonnay, Ca' del Bosco
Terre di Franciacorta, Ca' del Bosco

White Wines from the Friuli-Venezia Giulia and Trentino-Alto Adige

Chardonnay, Tiefenbrunner
  (Trentino-Alto Adige)
Chardonnay, Valdadige, Armani
Gewurztraminer, Alois Lageder
Lunelli, Villa Margon, Fratelli
  Lunelli
Pinot Bianco, G. Dorigo
Pinot Grigio, Armani
Pinot Grigio, "Collio",
  Borgoconventi
Pinot Grigio, Collio, Cantina
  Produttori, Cormons
Pinot Grigio, La Cros, Valdadige,
  Boscaini

Pinot Grigio, Rulander, Valdadige, S.
  Margherita
Pinot Grigio, Alois Lageder
Ribolla Gialla, G. Dorigo
Sauvignon, Collio, Dorigo
Sauvignon Ronco di Mele, Venica &
  Venica
Tocai Friulano, G. Dorigo
Tocai Friulano, Le Vigne di Zamo,
  Colli Orientali del Friuli, Rosazzo
  Manzano
Vintage Tunina, Jermann

White Wines from the Veneto

Ferrata Chardonnay, Maculan
Masi Bianco, Serego Alighieri
Soave, Bolla
Inama Soave Classico Superiore,
  Vigneti di Foscarino
Vespaiolo, Maculan

White Wines from Emilia-Romagna

Albana, Mario Pezzi

White Wines from the Marche (Marche)

Falerio dei Colli Ascolani, Saladini
  Pilastri
Verdicchio, Castelli di Jesi, Vinimar
Verdicchio, Cuprese
Verdicchio, Marchetti

White wines from Abruzzi (Abruzzo)/Molise

Trebbiano d'Abruzzo

White Wines from Sicily (Sicilia)

Bianco d'Alcamo
Marsala
Pinot Bianco, Corleone
Regaleali Nozze d'Oro
Zurrica, Abbazia Santa Anastasia

White Wines from Sardinia (Sardegna)

Moscato
Nuragus di Cagliari
Vermentino Sella & Mosca
Vernaccia di Oristano

White Wines from Campania

Falerno del Massico, Villa Matilde
Fiano di Avellino, Mastroberardino
Greco di Tufo, Mastroberardino

White Wines from Latium (Latzio)

Est!Est!!Est!!! di Montefiascone
Frascati, Gotto D'Oro

White Wines from Umbria

Cervaro della Sala, Antinori
Chardonnay, Lungarotti
Orvieto, Farina
Sauvignon, Castello della Sala,
  Antinori

White Wines from Tuscany
(Toscana)
 Galestro, Antinori
 Vernaccia di San Gimignano,
  Castelgreve di Pesa
 Vin Santo (sweet)

White Wines from Liguria
 Cinqueterre, Groppo Di
  Riomaggiore, Agricoltura Di
  Riomaggiore Manarola
 Linero Bianco, Vermentino,
  Tognoni
 Sciacchetra (sweet)

FRIZZANTE AND SPARKLING WINES

Frizzante Wines from Piedmont
(Piemonte)
 Red. Goj, Cascinacastlet, Barbera
  del Monferrato, Maria Borio
  Costigliore D'Asti, Nella Cantina
  Di Calamandrana.
 White. Asti Spumante

Sparkling White Wines from
Lombardy (Lombardia)
 Franciacorta Brut, Ca' del Bosco
 Vintage Franciacorta Brut, Ca' del
  Bosco

Frizzante Wines from the Veneto
 Tenutas Anna, Cabernet, Vino
  Spumante di qualita; a demi sec
  frizzante.
 Prosecco di Valdobbiadene, Cantina
  Produttori; a white frizzante

Frizzante Wines from Emilia-
Romagna
 Red. Lambrusco, Grasparossa Di
  Castelvetro, Manicardi

ROSÉ WINES

Rosé Wines from Sardinia
(Sardegna)
 Alghero, Sella & Mosca

Rosé Wines from Tuscany (Toscana)
 Rosato di Bolgheri, Antinori

To learn more about the training program, to make referrals for treatment for children, or to make a donation, please contact:

Toronto Child Psychoanalytic Program
31 Avis Crescent
Toronto, Ontario M4B 1B8
Canada
Telephone: 416-288-8689

ACKNOWLEDGEMENT

Luigi Orgera generously donated his recipes to the development of this cookbook, which is a fundraising project for training child psychotherapists and, thus, will contribute to the wellbeing of children. This training is provided by the Toronto Child Psychoanalytic Program (TCPP), Toronto, Canada.

The Toronto Child Psychoanalytic Program provides training in psychoanalytic child therapy with a four-year academic curriculum and clinical requirements for mental health professionals working with children and their families. The program was established in 1975 and there are currently more than fifty graduate child psychotherapists and over twenty-five candidates at various stages in the training.

The graduates provide psychoanalytic therapy to children who have serious emotional problems which, without intervention, can persist into adulthood, hindering emotional maturity and causing personality and relationship problems. The psychoanalytic child psychotherapists are deeply committed people who work intensively with children and their families.

Sally Doulis shops at a vegetable market in Palermo, Italy.

SALLY DOULIS, a food lover, is a social worker and psychotherapist who currently works in Toronto in the winter months and spends the summer with her husband sailing their yacht in the Mediterranean. In 1998, Sally Doulis was elected president of the Toronto Child Psychoanalytic Program.

COLLEEN MATHIEU, an accomplished cook, has been involved with food for several years. She is the co-author of *The Sable & Rosenfeld Cookbook – Our Favorite Recipes*. She is currently a consultant with Dinah's Cupboard Catering in Toronto.